Living Tradition

Living Tradition

Affirming Catholicism
in the Anglican Church

Edited by
JEFFREY JOHN

Introduced by
RICHARD HOLLOWAY

Darton, Longman and Todd
London

First published in 1992 by
Darton, Longman and Todd Ltd
89 Lillie Road, London SW6 1UD

ISBN 0–232–51981–1

A catalogue record of this book is available
from the British Library

Thanks are due to the following for permission to quote copyright
material: Faber and Faber Ltd, from the poem 'This Be the Verse'
taken from *High Windows* by Philip Larkin and from the poem
'Mutations' taken from *Collected Poems* by Louis MacNeice; The
Hogarth Press, from the poem 'The Church' taken from *Collected
Poems* by Edwin Muir.

The cover picture depicting Christ's command to Mary Magdalene
'Do Not Cling To Me' is a reminder that ours is a living tradition
because it is the expression of the living Christ: 'The Divine
Spirit . . . is forever breaking out of the prisons in which we try
to contain it, bursting out of the categories in which we entomb
it'. (p. 127)

Phototypeset by Intype, London
Printed and bound in Great Britain at the University Press,
Cambridge

Contents

Notes on Contributors

MOTHER ALLYNE CSMV was born and grew up in Australia and came to England in 1968. She entered the Community of St Mary the Virgin, whose Mother House is in Wantage, early in 1969 and took Life Vows in 1972. She was elected Mother of the Community in 1986.

ALAN BILLINGS is currently Vice-Principal of Ripon College Cuddesdon and Director of the Oxford Institute for Church and Society. Previously he was a parish priest in Sheffield and Deputy Leader of Sheffield County Council. He was one of the contributors to *Faith in the City*.

GEORGE CAREY became Archbishop of Canterbury in 1991. Previously Bishop of Bath and Wells, he has been a parish priest in Durham and Principal of Trinity College, Bristol. His books include *The Meeting of the Waters* and *I Believe*.

JACK DOMINIAN is a psychiatrist and the founder and director of the Marriage Research Centre at the Central Middlesex Hospital. His books include *The Capacity to Love*, *Sexual Integrity* and *Passionate and Compassionate Love*.

JOHN HABGOOD is Archbishop of York. His numerous publications include *Religion and Science*, *A Working Faith* and *Church and Nation in a Secular Age*.

RICHARD HOLLOWAY is Bishop of Edinburgh. He is the author of several books, including *The Killing*, *The Sidelong Glance* and *Crossfire*, and recently edited *The Divine Risk*.

JEFFREY JOHN was until recently Fellow and Dean of Divinity at Magdalen College, Oxford, combining the work of College Chaplain with research and teaching in New Testament Theology. He has now returned to parish ministry in South London.

ROWAN WILLIAMS has taught Theology at Mirfield, Cambridge and Oxford, where he is Lady Margaret Professor of Divinity. He has been a member of the Doctrine Commission of both the Church of England and the Church in Wales, and was consultant to the last Lambeth Conference. His books include *The Wound of Knowledge*, *Resurrection*, *The Truce of God* and *Arius*.

Introduction*

Richard Holloway

Recently I saw a Steven Spielberg movie called *Always*. It was a sentimental sort of film, discounted by the serious film critics. It was what Americans would describe as 'schmaltzy', but I watched it with a lump in my throat and a handkerchief at my eyes. A pilot who fights forest fires is killed saving his friend's life. He is sent back to earth to inspire and invisibly guide a young pilot who falls in love with his own grieving sweetheart. The film has a simple message. Before the hero can move on to the next stage in his pilgrimage after death he has to surrender his sweetheart to the young pilot and she has to stop clinging to the memory of her dead lover and move into the future. The film is about the delights and dangers of loyalty to those we have loved and lost.

Over the years I have noticed that loyalty is often a characteristic of church people, a loyalty that springs from gratitude. At some crucial and important point in their lives they received help, were tenderly ministered to, were loved – and they never forget it. If the event had spiritual or religious significance it becomes doubly important to them. At some point, through some agency, they were captured by the Divine, felt the gracious touch of God upon their lives.

Any number of people or things can be the agent of such an encounter: a beloved parish priest or Christian friend; a particular building, or corner of a building; a particular act of worship or passage of scripture. Whatever it was, through it God was encountered, love administered. Thereafter, the instrument through which the encounter was made will have a particular importance and to it a particular loyalty will be owed.

But these encounters with God's tenderness are not always sudden and precise, so that we forever remember the moment of encounter. Often it's like Henry Higgins' gradual realization, in *My Fair Lady*, that Eliza Doolittle is precious to him: 'I've grown accustomed to her smile,' he realizes. That's the way many people feel about the Book of Common Prayer or the Authorized Version of the Bible or traditional worship. They have grown accustomed to their beauty and are drawn through it to the mystery of the Divine Beauty. As a result, an intense loyalty develops, a sense of protectiveness towards the thing that conveyed the sense of God.

There's an obvious danger in all this. We have to ask ourselves, what was it that came through the transient moment, was caught for an instant in a beauty that vanished? It was a glimpse of God, a stirring of the Divine, and it answered our own heart's longing. But the beauty that captivated us, however fleetingly, came *through* the thing, it was not *in* it. Nevertheless, there is an almost inescapable human tendency to want to localize God, contain or limit God, to the people or places through which we have encountered the divine. When the Israelites were deported from Palestine to Babylon they thought they would never be able to know or worship God again, because he was back there in Jerusalem: 'By the waters of Babylon we sat down and wept, when we remembered thee O Zion. . . . How can we sing the Lord's song in a strange land?' (Psalm 137).

Another aspect of this human tendency to limit or localize God is slightly more surprising, but equally dangerous. Everything that was incidentally or accidentally associated with the original vision is treated as if it were equally important. The most profound example of this tendency is provided by the life of Jesus. According to Christian faith, God was revealed, was encountered in a unique way, in Jesus Christ two thousand years ago. Some Christians go far beyond the basic claim of faith and sanctify many of the attendant circumstances of that life. Jesus and his early followers were Jews, so for a time the early

2

Church thought only Jews could follow Christ. Closer to our interest is the status of women: because they were subservient to man in the society of Jesus' time, some claim they should be forever subservient. It is part of the human tendency to confine, limit, and localize the divine, so that we can keep it under our control. Our loyalty to the God we have known in the past blinds us to the new things he is doing in our own day.

This was the problem the disciples faced as the earthly ministry of Jesus Christ came to an end. Like Mary Magdalene in the resurrection garden, they wanted to cling to the earthly Jesus through whom they had learned so much about God. They had to learn a painful but liberating lesson. The divine is not by any of us to be bolted and padlocked on to any particular thing, so that when we lose that thing we lose God. That is to make finite things into God. The disciples were not even allowed to cling to the earthly body of Jesus. In order to know the Spirit of Christ, they had to give up, surrender, the Jesus they had loved so much. The divine Spirit cannot be buried in a particular liturgy, or tradition, or religion, or place, or person. It is forever breaking out of the prisons in which we try to contain it, bursting out of the categories in which we entomb it. This is the meaning of the Ascension of our Lord. The removal of Jesus from the physical realm meant that he was no longer limited by time and space. Now he was to be present to every generation. We are not to stand gazing back into history, mourning the dear dead past. We are to discover God in our own time and listen to what he is saying to us today. In other words, we must not let our loyalty to the past keep us from acknowledging what God is calling us to do in the present.

My meditation on these matters has been stimulated by reading Thomas Merton. I first read Merton as an impressionable Anglo-Catholic boy of fifteen. His autobiography, *Elected Silence*, fired me with its absolutism and search for submission to authority. I suppose it appealed to my own romantic longing to commit myself to some great cause, as well as to my adolescent impatience with mediocrity and uncertainty. At the time, I remember, it increased my youthful contempt for the Church of my birth, seeing it as a muddled compromise that lacked the drama and high clarity of the Roman Church. Merton's early writing from his monastery at Gethsemani in the mountains of Kentucky fuelled my 'Roman fever', but never quite brought it to the critical point. As my own understanding of theology, the Church and life deepened and became more complicated, I repudiated in my mind my infatuation with the early Thomas Merton. Nor did I keep up with Merton over the next thirty years. It was impossible not to be reminded of him during the 1960s, but my early experience had inoculated me against him and I refused to read the prophetic writings that poured from his pen. I rediscovered Merton in the 1980s, long after his death in 1968, and I experienced a mysterious recognition. This was still the Merton who sought absolute commitment and went on making his surrender to God, but there was a largeness and a generosity about his theological appreciation and spiritual vision that I had not found in his early writings. Here was a man who, by staying where he was, and listening and looking, praying and studying, had moved increasingly away from a fixed and authoritarian understanding of religion and had reached a point where, without diluting his commitment to the Christian way as found in the Roman Catholic Church, had yet developed a sympathy and a profound understanding not only of other Christian traditions, but of the non-Christian faiths, of which he had become a profound and sympathetic student.

I hope it is not too self-dramatizing to see a parallel between Merton's increasing impatience with, and distaste for, the authoritarian rigidities of the Catholic Church and of the Trappist order in which he was a monk, and my own depression over the state of the Anglo-Catholic movement in world Anglicanism and its increasing negativism and rigidity. It is loyalty that keeps us bound to the past long after we should have burst free. It is loyalty to the Catholic tradition in Anglicanism that has kept many of us from speaking out against its relentless opposition to anything that challenged the precise heritage of the past, especially in areas that concerned the emancipation of women to full freedom in the Church and certain contentious areas in the debate on sexual morality.

It was Merton as much as anyone, speaking from his hermitage in Kentucky in the early 1960s, who seemed to be speaking with the most immediacy to this situation. In his *A Vow of Conversation* we have his journals of the years 1964 and 1965. We share his meditation on what he is reading, as well as the result of his own prayer and contemplation. Early in 1964 he is reading Rudolph Bultmann. He tells us that Bultmann's essays are very revealing. 'He has made clear to me the full limitations of all my early work, which is too naive, insufficient except in what concerns my own experience.' Quoting Bultmann, he writes: 'Grace can never be possessed, but can only be received afresh again and again,' and, 'Man comes into his present situation as in some way under restraint, so that real freedom can only be received as a gift.' Then he goes on to say:

> One of the great temptations of an over institutionalised religion is precisely this: to keep man under the constraint of his own and society's past, so that this safety appears to be freedom. He is 'free' to return to the familiar constraint but this interferes with his freedom to respond to the new gift of grace in Christ. . . . Bultmann has a very real notion of tradition. Not a past in which to find a refuge.

Then he quotes Bultmann again:

> True loyalty to tradition does not consist in the canonisation of a particular stage in history . . . always criticism of the present before the tribunal of tradition but also criticism of tradition before the tribunal of the present day. *Real loyalty does not involve repetition but carrying things a stage further.*[1]

Ten pages later he tells us what all this means:

> I am aware of the need for constant self-revision and growth, leaving behind the renunciations of yesterday and yet in continuity with all my yesterdays. For to cling to the past is to lose one's continuity with the past, since this means clinging to what is no longer there.[2]

Of course, all of this is easier said than done but the living

Christ of the resurrection garden constantly calls us not to cling to our memories and traditions, but to leave the limits of the garden and follow him into the uncertainties of Galilee.

To hear this radical challenge has two consequences. The first is personal: we are to repudiate the seduction of nostalgia. Nostalgia cuts us off from the challenge of the present by turning our longing backwards to the irrecoverable and unrealizable past. Unhealthy religions do a lot of this, reminding us of the way things were, the purity and passion of the past compared with the corruption and tepidity of the present. They tell us that God's action and power are known only in the past, rarely in the present. But this is a kind of idolatry, because it makes God a fixed object. Merton, in his discussion with Jewish scholars, came to understand that idolatry is the basic human sin. He says that it is the sin of having a god who is other than he who cannot be made an idol, that is an object. We like God controllably locked in the past, because then we can safely objectify him and insulate ourselves against the unpredictability of the divine challenge. The other personal consequence of Christ's command to us not to look back is the unloading of our own guilt about past failure and sin. Guilt can also be a kind of idolatry, because it can be a refusal to accept the present power of God to cleanse and renew us. Forgiveness is the way we experience the presence of the living God in our lives, constantly drawing us away from the seduction of failure into the new future God has prepared for us.

The second major consequence for us of the command of Christ to follow him where he goes before, and not only to meditate on where he has already been, is the institutional or social consequence. All institutions, theologies and spiritual traditions can become idolatries, ways of making God a controllable object, rather than helping us to experience God as a living, unpredictable subject. This is why the Church and Christian believers need to be both penitent and hopeful. Expectation should be as much a part of our experience as repentance. Renewal should be as powerful an energy in the Church as forgiveness. We should expect God to do new things in our midst, as well as speaking to us through the inherited memory of what God has done for us in the past.

This book is about a particular example of the struggle to renew a tradition that had nearly hardened into idolatry, and seemed to have lost faith in a living and present God. It is about something that is happening in that corner of Christendom called the Anglican Church, but it should be of interest to people in other parts of God's house, because every attempt at human renewal has universal significance. The story begins in the Diocese of London in the mid-1980s. It was uncomfortable territory for men and women of the cast of mind expressed in the words from Thomas Merton that I have already quoted. There was a siege mentality abroad and the leadership of the Church called upon its members to repel hostile invaders, in the form of demanding women and new ideas about issues of equality in the Church and the status of minorities, including sexual minorities. The press was constantly telling us that the Anglican Church was in a state of terminal confusion, as traditionalists fought to expel the infidels from the city of God, in the form of an amorphous rabble, loosely described as liberals, wild creatures, allegedly of no settled theology or morality.

Of those days David Hutt, the Vicar of All Saints, Margaret Street, in London, has written:

> I can't recall the occasion – was it three or four years ago – when in the company of Alan Webster, then Dean of St Paul's, and Victor Stock, recently inducted as Rector of St Mary-le-Bow in Cheapside, that an idea was born. The London Underground in its present state is a mixed blessing but it does give an additional dimension to the metropolis. We were an unlikely trio but we had in common 'the Central Line'. Somewhere between our liberalisms and our conservatisms was a middle ground and there it was that we decided we should identify a meeting point and provide a meeting place for a number of friends and colleagues who literally had the care of the parishes on or near the Central Line Underground.
>
> From western suburbs to the East End we threw in suggestions and, with a good deal of licence, gathered some forty people in the drawing room of the Deanery. I'm sorry there is

no record of those gatherings – but an abiding image remains of Alan Webster, head in hands, eyes fast shut, speaking from some inner depth with eloquence and passion.

A number of useful things were achieved. The first was that, if not a 'safe house', then the Deanery was certainly endowed with the characteristics of an embassy within the London Diocese! We came by invitation and only what we found could justify the giving up of valuable mid-week time. For most of us this was sufficient, for it was here that we began to appreciate what was missing from our various ministries – the sense of belonging to something, of being valued, of being cared about. Following the main speaker, who had chosen a particular theme, the quality of discussion varied enormously and, looking back, I find it amazing that such a disparate body with all its hang-ups and expectations could meet and listen and laugh and share . . . The most obvious things in the world one might suppose, but the awful judgement is that most, if not all, came to tell of hurt and isolation – to 'tell their story' in a way totally authentic and deeply moving. None of this was self-conscious soul-baring or just whingeing for its own sake. We had given ourselves permission to speak as we did, to listen as we did and to find strength and encouragement in a way that we most certainly did.

The group was for ever changing and dates for future meetings arranged on a very *ad hoc* basis at the conclusion of each session. Not everyone stayed-on but somehow we went on meeting. Then came Alan's retirement and Victor and myself talked over what might be possible for the future. Among those who attended as frequently as most was Michael Mayne, Dean of Westminster. I wrote to him explaining the predicament and asking whether he would be prepared to provide a roof over our heads, as there was no guarantee that Alan's successor would be sympathetic to the philosophy of 'the Central Line' – non-partisan as it certainly was. He replied that he would be happy to do so provided we kept the name – which was useful and descriptive – and that he, although host and informal chairman, would remain very much part of the work of exploration and mutual support. We now had a 'safe house' with a vengeance, an undoubted embassy and even a kind of autonomous state within the Diocese!

Among the visitors to the group in 1989 was Richard Holloway, Bishop of Edinburgh. What he said at that gathering is of great significance because it provided the substance for what has become known as 'Tract 1990' (an allusion to Newman's 'Tract 90' of the last century). The text was submitted to the editor of the *Church Times* who printed it in an abbreviated form on 20 October 1989.

In that address I had offered a description, a sort of diagnosis, of the diseased state of Anglican Catholicism, and I went on to say:

I would like to suggest a programme of action. First of all, I think that unhappy Catholics in the Church of England must increasingly disagree with the present leadership of the movement. I know how painful this can be in terms of ostracism and repudiation, not to mention the receipt of unpleasant letters. Nevertheless, I think that Catholics, especially among the clergy, must increasingly come out of the closet and show what they truly think about many of the issues that confront the Church today. Secondly, we must argue, we must help Catholics to develop a theology of history and culture that enables them both to hold to the tradition from which they come and see that tradition as something dynamic and unfolding which is fed from the future as well as from the past. A commitment to a dialectical theology of this sort is spiritually perilous, but it is humanly unavoidable as long as we exist in time and not in a time-warp. Thirdly, I think we must emphasize and indeed celebrate the prophetic autonomy of Anglicanism.

We began by breaking step with medieval Catholicism and we must continue to refuse to be unequally yoked to any static or absolutist understanding of tradition. In Martin Thornton's language, tradition is a river as well as a rock, and while there is much we must guard, we must also commit ourselves to the exhilarating movement of history and play our part in discovering and being harbingers of the things that God has prepared for us. I think, finally, that we must break out of the purely protectionist mode of Christianity which we have occupied for years and go on the attack. While we are busily squabbling over whether a woman can receive the character of ordination, most of the country remains indifferent to the most basic elements of the gospel. If we are not careful, we shall decrease to the vanishing point while others increase. It is entirely conceivable that, given current trends in church growth, within fifty years the Anglican Church in these islands will be largely and rather narrowly evangelical in personality, and I think that the best of the evangelicals will admit that this is not a desirable future. We must develop an appropriate form of evangelism. Many of the early Catholic fathers were great evangelists, great preachers who called people to a living, converting relationship with Jesus Christ. Can we recover a proper evangelism that is non-manipulative, doesn't claim too much, and that really taps into the human need and longing for God? Much contemporary evangelism is manipulative, crass, cringe-making, guilt-inducing: can we discover an honourable evangelism that is filled with a longing for souls to meet Christ and to know God, and yet respects them and their integrity, respects their minds, their experience and wishes to affirm and not denounce their humanity? Can we find a modest, generous, yet passionate form of evangelism that will help us to share our pilgrimage with others?

To help us do all of these things I think we must organize. How many are we? And by 'we' I mean people who might once have called themselves liberal Catholics and who now might be happier to think of themselves as classical Anglicans, who seek to revere scripture, affirm tradition and champion reason in their following of Jesus.

One way to help such a recovery grow would be the mounting of a conference of interested people on whose agenda the following topics would be included:

An exploration of the dynamic nature of tradition and both the danger and the promise of theological development. What are the marks of a legitimate theology of culture that will enable us to discern the hand of God, not only in time past but in time present and time future?

How can we develop a new and indigenous liturgical aesthetic? We either seem to imitate Rome or submerge ourselves in the sort of minimalist liturgical banality of much contemporary evangelicalism. Can we do for our day what the ecclesiological movement did in the last century and in the early part of this century?

Can we struggle to discover an appropriate and honest evangelism that will help us to be faithful to the grand commission without setting the children's teeth on edge?

Can we tackle a whole range of thorny ethical issues, which currently bog us down, and find clear responses to homosexuality, to divorce and remarriage, to the political state of contemporary British society?

It's an exciting agenda and there are not a few of us who are anxious to get into it. Who will go with us?

That challenge elicited an impressive response. Most of the letters published in the *Church Times* were hostile to my diagnosis of Anglo-Catholicism as entrenched, negative and misogynistic, but I received 230 letters that were in entire agreement and expressed what can only be described as heart-felt gratitude. David Hutt described this outpouring as

the spontaneous testimony of men and women who responded with relief and told of their own isolation and increasing sense of despair at the stance of traditional Catholic leaders and organizations. It was as if a flood of pent-up frustration ahd been released simply as the result of one article in what is a very specialized journal with limited circulation. There is evidence that the text was circulated widely. This set a pattern for future pamphlets and articles which have been passed from hand to hand and provided material for discussion and debate.

The one firm result of the article and the response it elicited was a decision to accept an invitation from John Gaskell, the vicar of St Alban-the-Martyr, Holborn, in London, to hold a public meeting there. We were to begin an exploration of the agenda tentatively set forth in 'Tract 1990' on Saturday 9 June.

Many people wrote off my article as predictable. I was already known as a turncoat within the Catholic movement and my call, though it upset the traditionalists, did not surprise them. But in March 1990 the Vicar of All Saints, Margaret Street, that great shrine of the Anglo-Catholic movement not only in London but throughout the world, published an article in the *Church Times* called, 'It is Time to Shrug Off the Straitjacket'. In the article

David Hutt, an uncontentious man, with the bearing and politeness of a Sandhurst-trained officer of the British army, lifted his head firmly above the parapet and wrote:

> I am going to the Conference at St Alban's, Holborn, because, for me, the current agenda offered by Anglo-Catholicism is inadequate and incomplete. I want to hear as well as to be heard, contribute to a faithful Anglican engagement with reality, to love and to bless the past, but to do so knowing that both present and future are pressing and imperative in their demands.

Again, there was an outpouring of agreement and support. Typical of the letters received was one from Geoffrey Brown, Rector of St Martin-in-the-Fields, who wrote:

> There must be hundreds if not thousands of us who echo David Hutt's sentiments and feel that our loyalty to the Church of England stems from similar beliefs and attitudes. I want to stand alongside him in the hope that the flag he has flown will be a rallying point for all of us who feel bitterly let down by those who stridently claim that they speak the authentic words of truth and love, and yet hammer into the ground those who hold views different from their own.

In the event, more than two hundred people came to the conference at St Alban's, Holborn, on 9 June 1990, where Canon Rowan Williams set the tone of the day by pointing out:

> We are in a Catholic and a reformed Church; we believe that the real continuity of the gospel is sometimes served by apparent rupture and discontinuity . . . We ought to be able to manage a 'theology of disagreement' – understanding that our diversity is not primarily a mutual threat, but a mutual gift . . . We can afford to listen to each other, and to our cultural and intellectual milieu, not anxiously waiting to be offended but *expecting* to be taken somewhat deeper into the life of the living God.

Apart from the theological nurture the day offered, many people felt that it was a relief to have done the thing at all, to have found some means of letting out some of the pent-up tension and frustration we had felt, to have owned up to something in a public way, to have come out or shoved our heads above the parapet and found the view so bracing.

But more significant than that, perhaps, was the tone that was set. David Hutt wrote of the conference that, 'Friendliness overcame fear. There was no fear that day and Victor Stock's lively and idiosyncratic handling of the notices in his conference secretary's introduction frequently reduced us all to helpless laughter.'

It is this spirit of friendship and laughter that increasingly characterizes what has become known as Affirming Catholicism. It was the prevailing spirit of the full conference that was held in York in the first week of July 1991. The content of the conference is represented by the lectures published here for the first time, but they cannot capture the atmosphere of joy that was present throughout, in spite of occasional hitches in the organization and the surfacing of disagreement about the handling of this or that topic. The conference was a good cross-section of the Anglican Church. There were radical left-wing members of the Jubilee group present and there was at least one Thatcherite Tory, who entered into lively debate with them. There were women there who felt themselves to be refugees from a male-dominated institution and they told tales of hurt and insult. Present also were clergy who were uneasy about the ordination of women but who were determined to stay alongside them in their struggle. There were gay and lesbian Christians, who shared their pain and expressed their anger at what they perceived to have been systematic rejection, if not outright persecution by the Church. And there were also women in tweed skirts and sensible shoes from the Home Counties who had never met a gay person in their lives, or thought about the issues their presence represented. Painful issues surfaced about the role of gender and sexuality in the Church, the claims of tradition versus the call of God to listen to a new thing. But the really important thing about the conference was that it set a tone or an ethos. Several people said to me, 'This is what the Church should be like. A gathering of friends who are not afraid to show their wounds and share their disagreements, because they feel themselves to be affirmed in their weaknesses as well as in their strengths.'

We were affirmed too by the presence of the Archbishop of Canterbury who gave our opening address. His analysis of what he called the 'Catholic mosaic' and his answers to our questions reassured us of his own warm appreciation of Anglican Catholicism and his sensitivity to the issues we face as we try to renew and reinterpret it. We also realized how closely his feelings about his own Evangelical background – a mixture of love and exasperation with its more fundamentalist elements – mirrored our own feelings about Anglo-Catholicism.

That counterpoint of love and exasperation, reflecting the tension between continuity and development in the tradition, is a thread which runs through all the conference lectures as they focus on many of the separate elements in the Archbishop's mosaic. Rowan Williams speaks of Catholic doctrine as that which teaches 'the whole truth' about God and humanity, but reminds us that the way we express that truth is constantly, painfully evolving, because its inadequacy is constantly re-exposed by our perceptions of God's generosity and of the truth about ourselves. Jeffrey John highlights the questions which biblical criticism poses for contemporary Catholicism; but points out that the scripture itself is the record of a constantly changing tradition, and that our problems are nothing new. Alan Billings recalls the link between Catholic incarnational theology and social action, once seen in the Anglo-Catholic slum priests but now largely defunct, and suggests a new Trinitarian approach to a theology of social action for our changed society. Jack Dominian traces for us a psychology of personal development, and expresses his hopes for a renewed Catholicism that will help people to moral and spiritual maturity, not hold them down at the stage of infancy or adolescence. Mother Allyne of Wantage speaks movingly of the upheaval brought to monastic life by recent reforms, and of the many pains and challenges involved in changing a tradition from the inside; but states her conviction that after a necessary dying to aspects of the past a resurrection of the religious life is already powerfully stirring. Lastly, I concentrate on some of the particular problems we confront as Anglican Catholics today, with a reminder that turbulence is a sign of life not death, and a plea for a larger, more loving and confident Catholicism.

At the close of the conference we celebrated with a magnificent High Mass in York Minster, with the intention to ask God's blessing on what we have begun. Appropriately the Archbishop of York preached about the scope of tradition and development. He reminded us of what we must constantly hold in view: that the heart of our tradition, the unchanging heart which alone claims our ultimate and absolute obedience, is not any external formula, rule or dogma, but a living presence, the Spirit of Christ himself.

That, I believe, is the most important lesson we have to learn and to teach. There is a strong schismatic energy at work in our Church, on both sides of the Atlantic. The drive towards schism, the compulsion to create tidy, homogeneous ecclesial units of the usually angry and like-minded, is essentially anti-catholic and sectarian. The genius of Catholicism is not sameness, but universality, encompassability, the generosity that is inclusive, rather than the narrowness of spirit that is always looking for ways of locking people out. Of course, it follows that inclusive Catholic Christianity is more uncomfortable than exclusive sectarian Christianity. Let me speak quite personally: I am a passionate believer in women's ordination; I am a strong believer in revising the traditional Christian account of homosexuality; but, doctrinally, theologically, I am an orthodox, rather conservative Christian, who believes in the inspiration of scripture, who has little problem with the miraculous in Christian history (mainly because I believe in God's humour as well as God's compassion), who says his prayers, goes to Mass every day and makes his confession four times a year. Where do *I* belong? I refuse to be chased into some liberal Laodicean assembly where they will agree with me on sexual ethics and little else; nor do I belong among those who value the Mass, but do not seem to me to value the humanity of Christ as expressed in the pains and experience of gay men and women. No, I belong where I am, in a Catholic expression of Christianity that makes me rub against people I disagree with on some things and agree with on others. I need that largeness to challenge my intellectual and moral laziness, my tendency to intolerance. It is because of our cowardly temptation to retreat into little-nesss, into narrowness, that we need to be chased into the open spaces of generous Catholic Christianity. And we must struggle against the fear in all of us that would erect ring fences and brick walls to keep us from those with whom we disagree. Jesus came to break down all the walls that separate us, not to build them higher. During my lecture at the York Conference I quoted four lines of verse that seem to me to be the best reply to those who would divide the Church into exclusive sects:

> They drew a circle that shut me out –
> Heretic, rebel, a thing to flout.
> But love and I had the wit to win –
> We drew a circle that took them in.

For many of us the conference was a time of laughter and forgetting, but it was also a period of grace. Grace is the foundational element in Christianity, because it teaches us that nothing endures except the everlasting God whose gift supports the whole of our existence. Grace calls us to surrender ourselves wholly, without seeking some idol to hold on to. Through this thing that has started we have come to know the disconcerting grace of God with new power. It is characteristic of grace that it does not tell us where it will lead us. We shall follow it anyway.

1 Thomas Merton, *A Vow of Conversation* (Marshall, Morgan and Scott, 1988), pp. 6–7.
2 Ibid.

1 Revitalizing the Catholic Tradition*

George Carey

There are two major reasons for my affirming the Catholic tradition. The first is personal. Nurtured though I was in Evangelical Anglicanism, I have grown in my appreciation of the Catholic tradition: its vigour, its understanding of ministry, its colourful history, but perhaps above all, its spirituality. As a result I have become personally comfortable with your tradition without denying the Evangelical faith which first drew me into the Christian family. But I greet you too as an Archbishop of Canterbury who believes your importance is not limited simply to the history of our Church. Yours is a key witness if its future is to be healthy. I have no doubt that the integrity of Catholicism is vital for the well-being and future of Anglicanism. (I believe the same about the Evangelical tradition too, of course.) The decline of Anglican Catholicism – and there *has* been a decline even though some Catholics dislike acknowledging it – hurts us all. Its demise in the Church of England would be a tragedy.

And yet the gloomiest prophets see this as a real possibility. The reasons are manifold, and three years ago I charted some of them in an article in *Theology* on Church Parties.[1] Though not exclusively about the Catholic tradition, it was Catholics who responded most warmly to what I had to say. I remarked that the success of Catholicism in the Church of England is directly related to its decline as a movement. We are all aware of the remarkable revolution that the rediscovery of our place in Catholic Christendom has wrought in our Church. A mere hundred years separate us from the bitter disputes of the

Victorian era about regular Eucharists, the mixed chalice, vestments, auricular confession and so much else which is taken for granted by Anglicans today. I noted that partly due to its own success Anglican Catholicism seems to have lost its sense of direction these days. And indeed, its obsession with the single issue of the ordination of women seemed almost to indicate a death wish – a theological version of 'anorexia nervosa', a wasting away. The very existence of the movement, Affirming Catholicism, is a pertinent reminder to the Church that Catholicism stands for much more than a particular attitude to the ordination of women to the priesthood.

If there is one thing I regret about my article in *Theology*, it is its title, 'Parties in the Church of England'. Catholicism is always weakened by party spirit. Anything which restricts its vision or narrows its sympathies detracts from Catholicism's witness to the wholeness of the Church. Its contribution to Anglicanism has been a reminder that our Church forms part of a universal body of believers. Our communion with those outside Anglicanism may be imperfect but with them we share the Catholic creeds, the same scriptures, the apostolic ministry and that quality of the entire Church which is predicated by the term 'Catholic'. All that I want to say about Anglican Catholicism needs to be seen in the context of this wider vision. If Affirming Catholicism gets bogged down by simply creating another party in the Church of England, its mission will have failed.

Yet there is more to be said about the definition of Catholicism than I have done so far without narrowing its horizons. We need to hold on to the original meaning of the word 'catholic' in the epistles of Ignatius of Antioch, where it is an adjective qualifying the word 'church' and means a 'worldwide' body of believers. Later, 'catholic' came to mean 'orthodox' in distinction from those who deviated from the faith of the Church. Today it is a widely used term with as many meanings as those who claim it as their possession. But it is worth pointing out that, contrary to what many people believe, the opposite of 'Catholic' is not 'Protestant' but 'heterodox' or 'sectarian'. In its proper historical context the opposite of Protestant is not 'Catholic' but 'Papist'. The claim of our church to be 'Catholic and reformed' was and is no empty formula because our reformers did not reject Catholic faith; they wished a restoration of Catholic faith and practice. This is not, of course, to open up old wounds or assert old shibboleths. Roman Catholic, Anglican and Protestant theologians are now agreed in abhorring the bitterness that led to that split, whilst respecting the motives that led to all sides taking up passionate positions.

Yet whatever meaning people bring to Catholicism, it does represent a multi-layered theological, ecclesiastical and social mosaic which is of great importance to the Church. Catholicism in all its richness is vital for the progress of the faith in our land. Let me explore with you just some of the patterns of the Catholic mosaic.

First, Catholicism embraces a faith that is truly *incarnational*. This may appear to be an unexpected observation. It is not so to one brought up to view the Christian faith and life as stemming mainly from a theology centred on the death of Christ. Such a view sometimes leads to an other-worldly attitude to spirituality and to a didactic faith devoid of symbolism and beauty. Protestantism may lead, as we know well, to a dreary and dull attitude to life because the Christian hope is almost entirely projected into the future. In contract to this, Hilaire Belloc gave exuberant expression to the world-affirming qualities of Catholicism in his verse:

> Where'er the Catholic sun doth shine,
> There's music and laughter and good red wine.
> At least I've always found it so –
> Benedicamus Domino!

Belloc spoke, of course, for Roman Catholicism, but the vista painted is of a catholic view of life, stemming from the Incarnation of the Lord within the world, redeeming it by his life, death and resurrection, and thereby making it our home. The implication of this for ministry is obvious. A Catholic view of ministry has seen the incarnational spirit as pivotal for the exercise of a genuine priesthood, in contrast to other theologies. Thus the notion of

19

surrendering oneself to a ministry in a given place – to its suffering and gloom and death, as well as its joys and hopes – is rooted in a Catholic incarnational theology.

I was born in the East End of London. Although I am too young to know the great Anglo-Catholic Fathers of the East End – in Bethnal Green, Poplar, Stoke Newington, Bow – my parents regaled me with stories of their commitment, life and love. And since they were not regular church-goers, this shows the impact of these sacrificial ministries. I recall hearing about Brother Andrew who worked among the tramps and sang 'Count your blessings, name them, one by one' while innocently plucking fleas from his cassock, fully aware of the irony of the words! Of course, it is not only Catholic priests who live and work and die among their people. A Catholic incarnational theology does, however, see the action of God in and through the Son, who comes to be among his people, and is prepared to sacrifice all for their sake.

Within the Catholic mosaic there is a second element which is very closely connected with the incarnational, the sacramental principle. Sacraments speak of God operative and present through the visible, the tangible and the historical, indeed through the entire created order. Richard McBrien puts it in this way:

> The great sacramental encounter with God is Christ, and the Church, in turn, is the sacrament of encounter with Christ, and the sacraments in turn are the signs and instruments by which that ecclesial encounter with Christ is expressed, celebrated and made effective for all.[2]

The implication is that no thing and no person is ever outside Christ's presence and love. The infinite capacity of the Son to redeem, renew and restore is taken up by the Church's ministry and mission to declare the triumph of grace. I caught a glimpse of this last week at the Deptford Festival. A children's concert preceded the Mass. I was greeted with 'Consider yourself at home' as I entered the Church. Chinese children danced. There was more exuberant singing around the baroque altar. The local culture was being brought into church, celebrated and baptized. This was not an encounter with the Church on the

Church's terms. It was clear that the local community helped set the agenda too.

However, the sacramental approach itself is not without its dangers. These principally arise from the very openness which is its deep attraction. Hans Küng notes that if Protestantism might be accused of being too little or too narrow, then 'Catholicism cannot escape the accusation of being too much, a syncretistic collection of heterogeneous, misguided and even unchristian elements'. He goes on: 'There is a sin of *peccatum per excessum*, a sin of excess, as well as *peccatum per defectum*'.[3] The question then arises: What controls a tradition? On what basis do we say that a development is legitimate or illegitimate? Newman's ingenious attempt to justify development as a natural element of Catholic doctrine is not without its own problems, as Chadwick's *From Bossuet to Newman* shows so admirably. Principally, a so-called development may be so far from the original deposit of faith that it appears to be a new revelation.[4]

This directs us to a third element within Catholicism – namely its anchor in, and commitment to the original deposit of faith. Newman's doctrine of development, whatever its problems, is a testimony in itself to this. Even the earliest definitions of Catholicism against the heterodox views of Gnostics and others viewed the identity of the Church essentially in terms of its faithfulness to the *kerygma*; to the deposit of faith. The classical expression of it is found in the famous Vincentian Canon: '*Semper, ubique et ab omnibus*': 'What has been held everywhere, always and by all'.[5] The inclusiveness of this statement, taking in time and space, is very questionable, as Newman and others saw. It appeared to rule out the development of doctrine and dogma.

Whatever the difficulties over the development of doctrine, Catholicism is rooted in the historic faith of the Church. Its claim to be so is questioned only when it departs from the *regula fidei*, the Church's rule of faith. Our reformers were quite clear that the Reformation had made no new church but had merely restored catholicity to the Church by returning scripture to its rightful place

21

at the heart of the Church, and by making tradition and reason subservient to God's word.

However, where do we stand today when it seems that Catholic doctrine is in danger of being overthrown by new developments? This question is brought sharply into focus as our Church debates the issue of the ordination of women to the priesthood. No one feels more keenly than I the regrettable dilemma we are in; and this is not our dilemma alone, but the dilemma of all churches, for our pain is part of the pain of the entire Church of God. There is pain since our hopes and prayers for the unity of God's Church are threatened by this issue. Anglican Catholics – some of them anyway – have felt that unity with Rome was becoming a real possibilty, but that such progress as we have made will be lost. This is not the place to say whether their optimism was justified, but I do want to stress that those who appeal to the unity of the Church in the debate are not drawing our attention to anything we did not know. This is our pain.

On what basis then dare we as a church take such a momentous step as that of ordaining women? Some would say that we dare not and cannot do such a thing without damaging our claim to be part of the universal Catholic Church. But that argument has to be examined. Is it really the case that such a change must be submitted to the scrutiny of churches with whom we are not yet in communion before we can proceed? This is a novel argument even though those who propound it begin with an appeal to antiquity. Orthodoxy does not submit developments in its life to Rome before ratifying change. It is unlikely that the reforms of the Second Vatican Council would have taken place – certainly not as quickly – if Rome had waited for the approval of the Orthodox. Our reformers would have regarded the idea that major changes in the Church's life should await some General Council with complete amazement. It would have ruled out the Reformation itself. However regrettable you might think the Reformation, it is difficult to be an Anglican without recognizing its positive contribution to our understanding of Catholicism. William Wake, Archbishop of Canterbury (1717–37) said: 'The Church of England as a national church has all the power within herself over her own members, which is necessary to enable her to settle her doctrines, government and discipline.' To Dr Du Pin in Paris he wrote: 'In short the Church of England is free, is orthodox and has plenary authority within herself. She has no need to recur to other churches to direct her what to believe or what to do.'[6]

Of course this is not to say that we ignore the entreaties and the advice of other churches, but to quote Wake again: 'The truths of Christianity must not be sacrificed to the peace of Christians.' Here Wake was not arguing for some form of Anglican independency. He was no isolationist in doctrine or sympathies. The European links he established were remarkable for their breadth. What he emphasized, however, is that Anglicanism had preserved the deposit of faith in its loyalty to the scriptures, the creeds, the definitions of the General Councils, the threefold ministry and so on. Developments in its life would flow from those loyalties and be tested by them. The Church of England was no new creation, floating free from the rest of catholic Christendom. Faced by the issue of the ordination of women, the irony is that one group of Anglican Catholics now claims that the ordination of women may be a legitimate development within Catholicism while another group declares that it either is not or probably is not! Development, even in Newman's theory, was never achieved painlessly.

There is of course another pain we must recognize. This is the pain of women baptized into Christ who feel disenfranchised, marginalized and unheard. Our resolution of this matter must recognize the distress of both groups of people – those who feel such a development would call into question our Church's claim to be Catholic and those who feel they are not included in that catholicity simply because they are female. They believe that Catholics, above all, should witness to the wholeness of humanity in which arbitrary divisions between male and female have no place.

This brings me to a fourth exciting element in the Catholic mosaic – the notion of *wholeness* itself. For many Catholics this is linked with two things. The first is the 'whole'

23

Church. There are many Christians who regard the Church as simply a social entity; not so Catholics. For them it is an extension of God's being and life; part of the givenness of a sacramental understanding of faith. This gives to Catholicism a breadth and depth which invites Christians on a journey towards the fullness of faith. To use a phrase which I have gained from both Gerard Hughes and Rowan Williams, there is in Catholicism a capacity to be surprised. Catholicism, secure on its faith, has always encouraged speculative thinking. Its devotional life is strong enough to test it out; its traditions are secure enough to allow the Gamaliel principle to work. At its best, Catholicism creates an openness which produces possibilities for development as well as growth. Part of this journey is into the mystery of God himself, revealed as he is in Christ, but still capable of fresh understandings, new insights and undiscovered possibilities.

The other side of this is the 'wholeness' which the individual Christian seeks; the pathway of prayer, contemplation and praise. It is no surprise therefore to remark on the fact that the monastic and retreat movements, the desert Fathers, the great pioneers of mysticism and spirituality, derive almost entirely from the Catholic tradition of the Church. The Catholic style is seen most visibly and experienced most concretely here together with the hunger and drive for holiness without which we shall not see God. Of course, I do not wish to suggest that the tradition that first shaped me is and was incapable of teaching me to pray, to be silent, or to be holy. Far from it; the Evangelical tradition is firmly and passionately committed to a walk with the Lord, to living in the presence of God, to a holy lifestyle as the outworking of sanctification. But most unbiased Evangelicals will admit with me that the very immediacy of Evangelical spirituality seems to close off the growth of spirituality which is such a mark of the Catholic style. Central to that of course is the sacrament of the Eucharist, making available here and now the fruits of redemption, as the sacramental body and blood of Christ are taken afresh. Sacramental presence and sacramental adoration are hallmarks of Catholic spirituality, and part of the wholeness which the worshipper pursues.

A superficial observer might think that such a tradition would be so other-worldly as to be no earthly use. Far from it, and this brings me to a fifth part of the mosaic – Catholic social thought. Catholicism encourages a strong social conscience and a commitment to meeting the material needs of people. I have already referred to the Anglo-Catholic Fathers of London's East End, but one can think also of missionaries, like Bishop Frank Weston of Zanzibar, whose commitment to Christ led them into a radical obedience to his call to live among the poorest and to suffer with them. When a young priest bleated to Bishop Frank that he could not possibly live among savages in Africa, Frank growled: 'Who said anything about living. You can glorify Christ by your death, you know!' That deeply Evangelical-Catholic statement is more than a social gospel, it is the gospel expressed in dynamic action. It stems from the incarnational and sacramental principle noted earlier. I believe that ministry is still being expressed and lived out in our Church today by some priests, and we thank God for it.

But I would be doing Catholic social thought and action an injustice if I gave the impression that it was limited to the heroic work of a few priests. Catholicism has a social character because it emphasizes the corporate. People are saved by becoming members of the saved community, the Church. The individual is saved *in community*: that's why the question 'Are you saved?' is a foreign language among Catholics. 'There is no salvation outside the Church' is not a formula for institutional restriction on God's activity. It points to his grace at work in communities. Catholics believe that Christ's death shows the depth of God's love for every human soul – no matter how unlovely and unresponsive they may be. Christ's love was not theoretical: it was shown in his suffering, in his healings, his battle with all that disabled and handicapped the living of a full human life. Catholic social teachers used to make much of the sacramental principle working in more than one way. Social evils were, they said, the devil's sacraments

25

in which he communicated the deadliest of his poisons to alienate people from God.

The social mission of Anglican Catholicism has never been easy to distinguish from the last element of my mosaic – the evangelical spirit of Catholicism. The two have often been brought together in the life of religious communities. Anglican Franciscans, for example, have long referred to themselves as 'Catholic Evangelicals'. They, and other Anglican communities, have houses not only in the most beautiful of English countryside, but also in the midst of our inner cities and anonymous housing estates. Yet I hear few sermons urging the claims of the religious life. The fact that the Church of England has monks and nuns, friars and sisters, is one of our many well-kept secrets. Why be so quiet about it?

It was largely from our religious communities that the tradition of parish missions in Anglican Catholicism originated. I hear and see less of them now. The word 'mission' is avoided. Frequently the focus is on renewing the church congregation before we can evangelize more widely. As if we are ever going to get the gospel right before we preach it to others. The danger then is that we think we 'possess' the gospel and that gives rise to all sorts of terrible possibilities. I hope that the Decade of Evangelism will help Anglican Catholics recover their evangelical spirit, and I hope too that the religious communities will be at the forefront of this.

So, which way Catholicism? As Jeffrey John remarked in an excellent article last November:

> The truth is that for years now, since well before the present crisis, Catholicism in the Church of England has been dwindling from a movement into a ghetto. It has become increasingly introverted, negative, fundamentalist and fearful, and largely handed over teaching and evangelism – inside and outside the church – to the Evangelicals.[7]

That perception is uncomfortable but true. But it ought not to be. I want to affirm Catholicism and wish to suggest that you re-examine that mosaic of which I spoke.

If, as I have said, Catholicism has made such an amazing contribution to our Church, then perhaps the next step is to consolidate its life by affirming Catholicism in the traditions of others. The fullness of Catholicism, I remind you, does not lie in the Church but in the Lord of the Church. The Church only knows of the fullness of Christ. He is the fullness of Catholicism. No genuine Catholicism ever moves away from him but only *into* his fullness. Well did Hans Küng say – and I am passionately committed to this point of view – 'We need to replace a shortsighted and exclusive "Protestantism" and a diffuse and confused "Catholicism" with an "evangelical catholicity" based and centred on the gospel.'[8] Indeed, the challenge confronting Catholicism is whether it is Catholic enough to contain forms of Evangelicalism within it; just as the challenge facing Evangelicalism today is whether its gospel is genuinely Catholic.

Think again of the elements of the mosaic – an incarnational faith, the sacramental principle, the commitment to the *regula fidei*, the notion of wholeness, the tradition of social thought and action, and an evangelical spirit. All are linked. Catholic worship is in danger of becoming an empty ritual if the ministry which accompanies the celebration of the sacraments has no incarnational dimension. So give priority to the pastoring of the unchurched, and don't betray your tradition by setting sharp divisions between the Church and the world. Go in that direction and you will soon become a sect, losing your sense of wholeness, bereft of social action, and within an embattled rather than evangelical spirit. But what I don't want you to do is to neglect the deposit of faith. Listen to the strange saints of the desert, those puzzling early Fathers, and the voices of the Apostles. And, above all, attend to the word of scripture. Catholicism has always been suspicious of proof texts because you attend to the *whole* message of the scriptures. You pray it in the Psalms and the Offices. The God of the scriptures will always break free of any attempt to close him in a book, just as he will break free of any effort to imprison him in a tabernacle. For God will always surprise us by leading us into the fullness of truth. And he will always revive his Church with the waters of new life. In this Decade of Evangelism I pray for a vibrant Anglican Catholicism which will again feed the hearts and souls of God's people and lead our church deeper into the heart of the glory and mystery of our God.

In Edwin Muir's poem 'The Church' he speaks of a new Church about to open, and the blues and golds seem to speak of a new future. It ends:

> Yet fortune to the new church, and may its door
> Never be shut, or yawn in empty state
> To daunt the poor in spirit, the always poor.
> Catholic, Orthodox, Protestant, may it wait
> Here for its true estate.
> All's still to do; roof, window and wall are bare.
> I look, and do not doubt that He is there.

And I have no doubt that our Lord is here also.

1 'Parties in the Church of England', *Theology*, July 1988.
2 Richard McBrien, *Catholicism*, vol. II (Geoffrey Chapman, 1980), p. 1180.
3 Hans Küng, *The Church* (Search Press, 1968), p. 312.
4 Owen Chadwick, *From Bossuet to Newman* (Cambridge University Press, 2nd ed. 1987), p. 195.
5 See Paul Avis, *Anglicanism and the Christian Church* (T. and T. Clark, 1989), pp. 36–9.
6 Norman Sykes, *William Wake, Archbishop of Canterbury*, vol. 1 (Cambridge University Press, 1957).
7 Dr Jeffrey John in the *Church Times*, 9 November 1990.
8 Hans Küng, op. cit., p. 313.

2 Teaching the Truth*

Rowan Williams

We are all so used to hearing, and using, 'Catholic' as a term to designate a strand within a more complex tradition, a position among others, that we badly need to be reminded of where and how the word has its origins, and why it is properly an adjective qualifying 'Christian' – a word which opens up dimensions of our commitment to Christ, not a word which stands alone to claim another kind of loyalty. And if we are asked what it is to 'affirm' Catholicism, this *must* be where we begin to reply: not in terms of a *style* of being Christian, but in terms of certain necessary aspects of being a Christian at all. If we want to talk about 'styles', about particular emphases, at some stage, it must be in and from a concern about these aspects of being a disciple. If we care about the culture represented by the words 'Catholic' or 'Catholicism' – I mean the habits and disciplines and language of a particular bit of Christian history – it should be only because we believe that they hold the door open into these necessary dimensions of discipleship; and that means they are to be constantly tested against that understanding of discipleship. 'Catholic' Christianity has more, not less, of an obligation to be self-critical, if it takes the full meaning of the word seriously.

So: let me begin with the definition of 'Catholic' offered by a fourth-century bishop to the people he was preparing for baptism. In the eighteenth of his lectures to catechumens, Cyril of Jerusalem identifies five meanings for the word as applied to the Church. It is found *everywhere*: it isn't the religion of one race or group. It teaches the *whole*

*© Rowan Williams 1991

truth, all that people need to know for their salvation. It makes holiness possible for *all* kinds of people, rich and poor, clever and simple. It faces and deals with *all* the sicknesses and sins of human beings. And it displays the fullest possible *variety* of human excellence and every kind of spiritual gift. That is how Cyril teases out the meaning of a word whose root sense has to do with whatever belongs to the whole rather than the part; and what I find striking in these definitions is their concern with the variety, the crowded range, of human reality. If I were trying to paraphrase Cyril, I would say he is proposing that a Catholic Church is one which endeavours to *tell the whole truth* about God and God's human creation. And it is those two sides of Catholic identity that I want to explore here.

First, *telling the whole truth about God* – teaching 'all that human beings ought to know about things visible and invisible', in Cyril's words. We may think of those breezy little books offering 'all you need to know' about computers or beer-making or whatever: as though 'all you need to know' automatically meant 'just about enough to manage'. But it is fairly clear from the way Cyril speaks that he is coming at the question from the opposite end: 'Catholic' teaching is what keeps nothing back, leaves nothing out that could contribute to our healing. Ours is not a faith in which some things are carefully reserved for the élite, but one in which truth is public and accessible, in which people are trusted to be allowed to approach God as God is, not held at arm's length by professionals dealing out carefully rationed quantities of information. This obviously connects with some of the other things Cyril has to say: this is not a faith for specialists, but opens up something for all. Neither we nor God have to be protected from each other.

The very enterprise of telling the whole truth about God in fact tells us already something of the kind of God we speak of: a God who holds back nothing, who is not jealous of creation, or self-protective. Another fourth-century writer, tackling the question of why it is difficult to talk about God, wonders whether it is because God (like the classical deities of Greece) is reluctant to expose the mysteries of the divine nature for fear of endangering the dignity proper to God; and he promptly answers himself – quoting Plato – that God cannot be envious, and so cannot be ungenerous. God is God, and so needs to safeguard nothing because the divine life can't be endangered or diluted. So the God who entrusts us with speaking the truth is one we already know to be generous without reserve and dependable without change, who is free to set us free, whose proper name is indeed 'I will be what I will be'. In that vision, all talk about God begins and ends.

But it means that talking of God can be chaotic. It is not to be restricted to those possessed of authorized information (which is why this dimension of being Catholic should make us look long and hard at the endemic clericalism of those – us – who call themselves Catholic); it will not necessarily obey the rules of careful secular prose; it isn't *meant* to be glibly economical or even argumentatively impeccable. The first event in the public history of the Christian community was an outbreak of baffling, noisy, exuberant talk in diverse languages; and the great moments of the Church's renewal have all been associated with new words for praying and singing, new images, a new liberty to open one's mouth in confidence. From the Reformation to the Methodist Revival to the charismatic movement to the Bible study in the Latin American base community, renewal has meant people, all sorts of people, finding authority to talk *of* God and *to* God. We may find their words odd – we, on the whole safe, reasonable and careful people, God help us – but the moment at which a person senses for the first time that he or she has the liberty for such speech should be for us a moment of revelation, of truth-telling about a God who risks the divine truth in opening the mouths of fallible people; because to be God *is* to be the generosity of self-communication.

Catholic talk about God needs to give space to all this, and to be able to hold on to a wide range of idioms for speaking of and to God. If it is aware of a heavy responsibility for maintaining and transmitting some of the forms of past ages – a responsibility that can make would-be Catholic language look fussily antiquarian and tribal at its worst – it is surely because of a conviction that this or that way of speaking of and to God has done something substantial for the healing and maturing of human beings. There is no justification for sneering at the theology and liturgy of other eras: we needn't always endorse it, but we *do* need to have some imaginative sense of why and how it mattered, and how it transmitted the gospel. But this brings us to the rather thorny issue of doctrinal statements and their binding quality. Can we combine a generosity about the range of idioms used by Christians with a commitment to believing that it is indeed *truths* we are struggling to tell? I have to confess that I suspect the difficulties here have been a good deal exaggerated. At the most simple level the very attempt to talk of God in the way Christians do presupposes a truth about God – divine freedom, divine generosity. And as soon as you grant that you make a doctrinal claim, a claim that there is truth to be taught about God. The existence of new, distinctive patterns of life and language, from Pentecost onwards, constantly poses the question of what it is about God that would make sense of all this. The slow and difficult evolution of a doctrinal language, creeds and definitions, is a witness to how that question is dealt with; and, broadly speaking, definitions represented by our creeds and by the general shape of our common worship have to do at heart with maintaining the possibility of speaking about a God who becomes unreservedly accessible in the person of Jesus Christ and in the life of Christ's community. What is rejected is, pretty consistently, any teaching that leaves God only provisionally or partially involved in the communicating of the new life of grace and communion. Never mind for the moment whether the rejections of early 'heresies' were based on entirely fair judgements: scholars will argue long and fiercely over this. What is clear is that the doctrinal statements of our formative centuries reflect the pressure of a single vision – of the God who holds nothing back. And if we want to teach Christianity truly, we need to be able to make the connection between the language of creed and worship and the fundamental recognition embodied in the fact of trying to talk about God at all.

Need we bother, though? The question still gets asked by those for whom 'liberalism' itself becomes a tight orthodoxy, in their concern that people will be made anxious by complexities or by pressure to accept the incomprehensible (this is when we start hearing nervous jokes about the Athanasian Creed). But there are at least three things that can be said in response. First, beware of being sentimental about simplicity. In all kinds of ways, reality *is* complex, and it is foolish to pretend otherwise. Whether that complexity comes across as intimidating or enriching depends a lot on how and in what context it's communicated. Secondly, beware of patronizing – the wrong kind of 'all you need to know' approach. If the human mind is capable of being stretched in the arts and sciences into the vision of truths not easily and quickly mastered, we have no business saying that tracing the logic and connections of God's dealings with us and asking how we can least stupidly talk of God in the light of all this is just too demanding or time-wasting for the 'ordinary layperson'. This is élitist nonsense. Of course there is a history of authoritarian mystification, of people being told to believe what they were not expected to understand; but it's no use colluding with that by the claim that real Christian truth does not or should not challenge the mind and imagination as well as the heart and will of every believer. And third, it is worth remembering that doctrine can be pressed into the service of inhuman and unchristian oppression – that it can be a tool of corruption and violence. The less people are enabled to take responsibility for grasping the shape of the world they stand in, the shape moulded by a self-sharing God, the more readily the distortion and manipulation of Christian rhetoric can have its way, whether in the anti-semitism of a French or Polish Catholic reactionary or in the bland pieties of Reagan's America; or nearer home.

But beyond all this is something further, more solid but more elusive. The truth about God is a truth to be enjoyed. Trying to tell the truth about God can take us, it seems,

33

a good way from what we might *think* we need to know in order to lead reasoned and happy lives; it can draw us into bold reflection (the word 'speculation' is a bogey here) which, of course, runs the risk of becoming an end in itself. But it will not do this if its aim is to see and to show a reality that is *wonderful*. Our tradition has laboriously worked round to recognizing that the life of God is movement, exchange and mutuality, the life of the Trinity; it has wrestled with what is meant by discerning in Jesus the unsurpassed presence of one moment in that everlasting exchange, discerning the incarnation of the Word; it has struggled in word, image and ritual to say what is involved in the conviction that the spirit of Jesus in the community makes the stuff of the material world transparent to God's act, the conviction of sacramental grace. It has done all this ultimately with the delight we might have in looking again and again at a picture or a drama that has moved and changed us, enlarged our world, seeing more and more dimensions and connections.

To put it bluntly, Christian doctrine is not just useful, it is beautiful. If we cannot give thanks for God's great glory, the glory of the eternal Trinity, the glory of God in the face of Jesus Christ, it will not be even useful for long, because it will not compel and involve us. Moralism with a sentimental gloss of mythology does not, as far as I can see, radicalize our perception of each other very deeply for very long. Knowing a little of what the image of God in us might mean is likely to make us more lastingly and obstinately outraged at the desecrations of human violence: the image of God in the incinerated face of the Iraqi soldier on the Basra road just as in the face of the victim of the régime he died fighting for, or the abused child in care, or the convict in prison, or the victims of military terror and nationalist fanaticism in Yugoslavia. Telling the truth about God is uncovering a beauty that is *terrible* because we shall not be able to help seeing what we do to it: without the joy, no saving anger or shame or penitence.

But talking about wonder reminds us too of the most sobering aspect of trying to tell the truth about God. Telling the whole truth here is telling also what we *cannot* say. Because of the nature of what we speak of, God's liberty, we do not come to an end. And when doctrinal language or the language of preaching and worship has become sterile or has come to be seen as a tight and adequate scheme, we have to learn the divine freedom all over again by what silences and disorients us, by the recovery of whatever it was that on Easter morning sent the first witnesses of the resurrection away afraid to speak because, like Paul, they had heard what they had no words for that were not empty. The shrewd philosopher observes that when I say 'I can't tell you how grateful I am', I am telling you how grateful I am. And the hymn writer who begins, 'How shall I sing that majesty?' sings it in those words.

When we find ourselves clinging to formulae (whether 'conservative' or 'liberal') and no longer asking whether the way we use them actually speaks about the transformation worked in Jesus Christ, we are desperately in need of something – in our culture, in our individual experience – that makes us inarticulate. Because there are times when we can only speak of God by the awkward, impotent recognition that we have not yet found out what our words are really about – the recognition of what is not said or seen, of an excess of reality over what we think we know. Bonhoeffer in 1944 could write about how the moral collapse of the German churches, even those trying to resist the Nazi state, indicated that Christians did not really know the meaning of 'great' words like 'redemption', 'regeneration': we would have to wait to rediscover a language capable of changing the world, and meanwhile be content with prayer and the struggle for just action. Thomas Merton's extraordinary spiritual pilgrimage is punctuated by moments of bewilderment and even disgust with the language he had learned to use so well. In his last published journal, describing the beginnings of his life as a hermit, he writes of the constant rediscovery of being before God in the concrete business of his life: 'What matters in our life is not abstract ideals but profound love and surrender to the concrete judgements of God.'[1] These are not people bored or disillusioned with Christian doctrine ('too complex', 'too abstract'); this very journey

35

into prayerful attention, mindful presence, is informed
throughout by the vision and the narrative of the Christian
God. They have simply recognized that doctrine is a set
of instructions for performance.

– Tell me about God.
– Watch.
– What does the doctrine of the Trinity mean?
– Watch.
– Why should I confess that Jesus is Lord?
– Watch.

'Mindful presence'. To God, yes, and then – or rather
simultaneously – to the world. And so to the second
dimension of catholicity, *telling the truth about humanity*, so
that all sorts of people may become holy and all kinds of
sins and injuries be healed. The risk we run in believing
we have good news for all persons and situations is to
turn that into a general formula – which means setting up
a sort of abstract, universal person as our ideal audience;
as if, when Paul says that there is in Christ neither Jew
nor Greek, slave nor free, male nor female, he means that
instead of actual human beings (who are obstinately and
irreducibly Jews, Greeks, slaves, etc.) there is, for Christian purposes, a single standard-issue subject. Do you
remember the story of the mad Cornish parson (one of
many) who kept the church locked and filled the pews
with cardboard cut-outs? A remarkable parable of what
we do in losing sight of the particular and solid reality of
those we want to hear the gospel. If we recognize what I
can only call the *density* of actual human lives, two things
immediately become obvious.

The first is that we are not in control of where people
are. A lot of our moral talk goes on as if the world were
meekly waiting for Christians to tell them what to do
(and as if Christians in general were meekly waiting for
bishops, synods or theologians to tell them what to do);
and meanwhile the Spirit of God moves upon the face of
the waters, or something, and *nothing actually happens*. But
of course things are happening. We are *always* dealing
with the legacy of lives already lived, decisions made,

injuries given and received – which is what I mean by the 'density' of lives. And to have a sense of what this means demands of us a level of patience and attention that can properly be called 'contemplative'.

How are we to learn how to speak what we believe to be good news to someone without listening for their language – which means listening for their particular histories, their otherness and strangeness? Simone Weil wrote that the heart of a moral relationship to other human beings was 'hesitation': we recognize the reality and dignity of another, the fact that they are not abstract fictions of our own preference, in the degree that we pause to look and to hear before we impose solutions, interpretations, condemnations or whatever. Just as in our relation with God our not knowing what to say may be what speaks most eloquently *of* God, so with others, the moment of hesitation, the patience of attending, *shows* what might be meant by believing that women and men are in God's image. 'One approaches these souls', wrote the great English Jesuit Cyril Martindale in 1912, 'with, O, infinite respect, affection, slow study, self-distrust and, more than all else, prayer (because, left to oneself, one will remain a clumsy, meddlesome mischief-maker to the end of one's days).'[2] Martindale was writing about school-teaching, but I don't need to labour the point of the wider application. (And think for a moment about what schools might be if these were the assumptions of those who organize our educational system.) We are not in control of the otherness of others; we – whatever our own proper confidence and authority – must learn 'hesitation'.

A second point, then: you cannot articulate a moral and Christian judgement by speaking in a way in which you could not speak if the object of your judgement were actually *there*. Let me explain. One of the things that is, I suppose, most offensive about racist jokes (for example) is the implicit assumption that the target is not and really could not be there in the audience, and *we*, enjoying the complicity of this little like-minded group, allow ourselves to fix, limit, diminish the humanity of those excluded. Well, think for a moment of conversations, private and not so private, in Christian circles of which this might be

said. We can and we do discuss the remarriage of div-
orcees, the ordination of women, the ethics of homosexuality, the representation of black Anglicans in Synod,
consistently as if the people being talked about were not
really there and could not be – could not be partners in
this conversation because it is assumed that their voice has
nothing to contribute. (Oh, and before we congratulate
ourselves too warmly, I have to say that you do hear
conversations about people opposed to women's ordination, etc., which have the same quality of exclusive
complicity.) How on earth do we learn to speak about
these matters and these *persons* as if they were *present* to
us? This is not rambling from the theme of catholicity, for
surely the most uncatholic thing we can do is to tailor
what we say for a limited range of people, for the public
faces of those we think we get on with. But public faces
are so often a hall of mirrors – I show you what you want
to see, you show me what I want to see – and the truth
of human difference fades away.

A lot of our private and corporate human life struggles
towards the goal of eroding differences, as if the common
life were indeed the life of nobody in particular. And this
has something to do with how hard it is to face the really
unresolved and unhealed character of so much human
experience. It is not just that we are frightened by each
other's otherness – though it's true that we are. We are
also frightened by the idea that there are pains we cannot
cure and knots we cannot untie. The uncontrollability of
other people, in this connection, comes over as our own
powerlessness to make order out of human lives, including our own.

Here, though, it is worth remembering all those
elements in Catholic tradition that ought to help us with
such a recognition. Catholicism has always taken seriously
the *process* of sanctification. In the disciplines of confession
and direction, it takes for granted that the forming of
Christ in a human life is a lifetime's work, a constant
discovery at ever deeper levels of our resistance to God's
love. From St Augustine onwards Catholics have watched
with interest, irony and compassion, the sheer uneven-
ness of the processes of growing into Christ. It is no

accident that so many of the novelists who have most powerfully depicted the endless resources of self-deception and the sheer human unlikeliness of sanctity have been formed by Catholic Christianity (Waugh and Greene, obviously, but also, in differing degrees, Iris Murdoch and Alice Thomas Ellis and even P.D. James; or in the USA J.F. Powers and Flannery O'Connor and Walker Percy, Mary Gordon and André Dubus). It cannot be said too often – even at the risk of sounding middle class – that the perception of the image of God in people and the nurturing of contemplative hesitation needs, and feeds on, a vital cultural life, in which the attention span for human interaction is more than the three minutes allowed by soap opera.

Here I am reminded of the fourth and last of Alan Bleasdale's first series of television plays about Liverpool, *George's Last Ride*. In the old socialist docker, Bleasdale creates a rare portrait of authentic holiness (not just decency), with, at best, a pretty tenuous link to his Irish Catholic roots. At George's requiem, the priest, bored and tired and pathetic, gets George's name wrong and begins a set of dutiful and untrue platitudes about his Catholic virtues. He is interrupted by a young, troubled, unemployed friend of George's, who tells him he is not speaking the truth: the church is full not because of George's Catholic virtues but because people are thankful for a goodness visible to anyone with eyes to see. The priest is shaken by this outburst (we are allowed later to see his own pathos, drunk and retching at the wake), and says that 'obviously the Church has nothing to say here'. A haunting moment: the priest is right in one way, and there is humility in that; he knows when to be silent. But the Church which is *not* the official and bored voice has already said what it has to say, affirming the 'density' and particularity of a holiness that has escaped the tribal prison.

Catholicism teaches us patience with the windings of the soul and disciplines to trace them and point them to Christ; but it needs also to acknowledge God's liberty to take time with souls beyond the structures of the Church. When we fail to speak to and to nourish the protesting, the doubting or the injured, God can be more catholic than we are. It is the worst possible commendation of our faith and of the grace it brings to be slow and ungenerous in recognizing that God's work of bringing Christ's life is there ahead of us in the world. But any pastor, or indeed any Christian with any sense, will say as much.

Sanctity, which is what we are all called to, does not happen to persons in the abstract. One of the most alarming criticisms of the disciplines of Christian spirituality and education, often made, is that it requires simple denial of what we know to be true of ourselves – I mean not only aspects of our sexuality, but all sorts of twists and turns of vanity and self-serving and half-instinctive malice, which can be clothed in terms of religious excellence. If our own reality, our own 'dense' particularity, is to be made holy, we have to confront all these.

This leads to one last thought about truthfulness with respect to humanity. Attention, hesitation, listening – all these *can* be taken, by a superficial observer, as weakening our sense of the reality of sin. Many people will inevitably sneer at any version of the gospel which makes much of patience and acceptance, as if this meant no more than inexpensive tolerance. But part of the point of attention and listening is to see clearly – in myself, in others, in my society – where the tangles of resistance and destructiveness really are. There is no Catholic discipleship without repentance: we are brought to Jesus Christ for judgement and for healing; we are to be shown uncomfortable truths. A policy of acceptance for its own sake would divorce our relations with one another from our vision of God, which tests, discriminates and wrestles with what opposes its own integrity. It is a difficult path to tread: the trouble with glib moralism is that so often it ignores the complex and extended nature of human growing, ignores the fact that we never begin in a vacuum. The trouble with some sorts of 'affirmative' approach ('creation spirituality' in some of its more simplistic versions) is that they are no less glib and impatient and insensitive to the complexity of persons. There are moments when I am tempted to think that the only useful and honest moral discourse is in the context of confession or direction, when the particularities of experience are brought slowly into connection with the communally-confessed truth of God's nature and activity.

But that is to say that the business of Christian education and formation has a lot to do with enabling people to reimagine their lives *in relation* – in relation to God and to God's people. I have talked about 'mindful presence' as the foundation of our moral communication, and about the goal of this communication being to make connections between a particular experience and a global vision of God's dealings. Perhaps, then, we can pick up an idea much used by modern Eastern Orthodox writers, and talk about the formation of 'Catholic personality'. Our life in the community of Christ produces a style and sense of human identity that takes us definitively beyond individualism. We assume all along that we as individuals in isolation do not apprehend the truth. It is in the giving and receiving of Christ's loving attention that we become persons who know and who live in truth. And the Catholic Church is, in this perspective, the Church of catholic persons, listening patiently and expectantly to each other, and in this exchange being brought towards the truthfulness of Christ (judgement and promise), discovering more deeply the spring of their common life, how the one Christ appears in the real diversity of many lives.

The political witness of the Church is rooted here too, in this sense of how diverse persons and communities need one another for their life and so need to be free to give to each other (the freedom which class hierarchy, nationalism, obsession with military security, and racial injustice constantly threaten). It is the *fact* of the Catholic Church's existence – persons and groups set together for learning, nourishment, challenge – that remains the corner-stone of a social vision, not abstract principle or even the 'bias to the poor' on its own (though such a bias is precisely how the Catholic vision becomes tangible in a situation of dominance and inequity). We have the awkward but stretching task of combating both the lazy and arbitrary individualism of most of our culture and the abstract generalities of moralist systems, what C.S. Lewis dubbed 'pseudo-theologies of both Left and Right'.

41

Telling the truth about both God and humanity is thus, predictably, inseparable from becoming holy: enacting our doctrine, realizing that doctrine itself is simply the deposit of a transforming of relationship to God and God's world. We shall tell the whole truth if we continue to be a church in which saints are made – and I think we need to hold on to that as fundamental, whatever our anxieties about this or that cause or movement. I am not suggesting we can resolve all our conflicts by this means: precisely *because* we are particular, not abstract, persons, we have commitments which we make and sustain in the conviction that we are furthering God's will. (Whenever I'm tempted to impatience with the dogmatism of my opponents on an issue like women's ordination, I have to remember to look at my own anger and bitter frustration and sense of betrayal by my church over the question of war and peace. I am not pretending it doesn't hurt to live with rival commitments.) But the reason for being faithful to the Church must finally be that we can point to lives in which the full truth of God is visible and in which we see what the 'Catholic person' might be. Faithfulness to the Church is hopeful, then; it looks to human beings for glory and promise, but without illusion. Expecting holiness in one another is not a matter of optimism. It is what we learn by discovering in ourselves that repentance constantly opens us to an inexhaustible source of mercy and nurture. We do not come to expect holiness without acknowledging failure and injury, nor can we cope with the full disturbing recognition of our failure and injury without the expectation that God will make us whole if we let God do so.

And that brings us back again to the fundamental confession of God's freedom with which we started. On this the whole Church rests; in this faith is the possibility of a voice and place for all. I do not think Affirming Catholicism will get very far if it fails to go on affirming our needs (ours, not 'theirs') to be reconverted daily: to contemplation of God and contemplative patience with men and women; to the pain of seeing God's image defaced in our prejudice, apathy, lies and violence (as a society and a Church) and the positive anger coming from that; to repentance; to the 'Catholic personality'; to a truth which, please God, our life together will teach.

1 Thomas Merton, *A Vow of Conversation* (Marshall, Morgan and Scott, 1988), p. 165.
2 Philip Caraman, *C.C. Martindale, A Biography* (Longman, 1967), p. 119.

3 Making Sense of Scripture*
Jeffrey John

The problem with the Bible

At school we had two R.E. teachers; they were called (let us say) Mr Evans and Miss Tomkins. These two approached their task in bewilderingly different ways. The senior, Mr Evans, was a Welsh Methodist of the old school, and a part-time preacher. For Mr Evans, his Bible was his religion and his religion his Bible; and he believed the Bible in its most plain and fundamental sense. He believed it literally and unquestioningly, and had they but been mentioned in its pages, he would have believed in leprechauns, King Arthur and Father Christmas as well. At least with Mr Evans you knew where you stood. Miss Tomkins was a different kettle of fish. She was an Anglican, and had 'modern' views; I think Mr Davies regarded her as Jezebel and the Whore of Babylon rolled into one. Miss Tomkins had been in the Student Christian Movement at university. She had read modern books by modern theologians like Bishop Robinson; and such books had inflamed her with the idea that you had to make religion relevant to the youth of today. Miss Tomkins' main method of being relevant was to dismiss anything that sounded supernatural as being 'primitive' and 'unscientific'. Her great speciality was demolishing miracles. If Mr Davies told us about the parting of the waters at the Red Sea, Miss Tomkins would tell us it was all to do with winds and tides and sandbanks, as if you could walk through the Red Sea any old day. If it was Moses' snake turning into a stick in front of Pharaoh, she would tell us snakes like that are two a penny in the Holy

*© Jeffrey John 1991

Land, and look just like sticks when they're frightened. When we came to the raising of Lazarus, she told us about cataleptic fits, which make people seem dead when they are not. And when Jesus healed the sick, it was 'psychosomatic' she said. She loved the word 'psychosomatic'. In fact, if Miss Tomkins was right, the incidence of psychosomatic deafness, dumbness, blindness and leprosy in first-century Palestine was a miracle in itself.

I recall both teachers telling us the story of Jesus Feeding the Five Thousand. With Mr Evans there wasn't a great deal to say. 'Well, it's a miracle, isn't it?' he said. 'It goes to show Jesus is God, and God can do what he likes.' 'Miracle my foot!' said Miss Tomkins the following week. What *really* happened, she said, was that Jesus and the disciples shared out their own loaves and fishes with the people nearest them, but then lots more people around, noticing this wonderful example of unselfishness, suddenly remembered that they had brought their lunch boxes with them and were inspired to share what they had too. So out came the sardine sandwiches they had been selfishly hiding all along, and then of course there was more than enough to go round! 'The *real* miracle', said Miss Tomkins, 'is that if only we care and share with others, the world will be a better place.' Edifying as this was, I don't think it struck us as particularly miraculous, or particularly good news.

The alternatives of Mr Evans' fundamentalism and Miss Tomkins' reductionism produced in me an active dislike of the Bible, and a strong feeling that only rather stupid people bothered with it. This was reinforced by the school, which lumped scripture in with art and woodwork, and only let you do it for O-level if you were in the 'B' stream. So in the fifth form I abandoned scripture with a happy heart, and at the same time I abandoned my Nonconformist heritage and got confirmed, much to Mr Evans' disgust, in an Anglo-Catholic church near home. For me one of the positive attractions of Anglo-Catholicism was that you didn't have to worry about the Bible. You heard bits of it at Mass of course, preferably sung with incense and candles, but didn't pay it much attention. Preachers usually took a quick glance at the readings of the day, then passed on to talk about confession or the annual pilgrimage to Walsingham or wherever else the real interest lay.

A few years later, reluctantly preparing to start a theology degree so that I could get ordained, I began my preliminary reading with Dennis Nineham's commentary on Mark.[1] Strange as it may seem to you, to me this was a Damascus road experience. For the first time I discovered that instead of having to shut off my brain like Mr Evans to pretend the gospel was simple history, or instead of having to reduce it, like Miss Tomkins, to a source book of moral fairy-tales, here in Mark was a work of astonishing depth and subtlety whose real nature I had never guessed, and whose layers of meaning one might spend a lifetime attempting to plumb.

Let me take the Feeding of the Five Thousand as an example. I told you what Mr Evans and Miss Tomkins made of it. What I learned from Nineham was this. First and foremost, whatever history may lie behind it, this story, like the whole gospel, has to be approached as literary creation with a theological purpose. Perhaps its most obvious aim is to tell us that Jesus is the new Moses. Like Moses Jesus crosses the water into the desert, like Moses he sits the people down and feeds them with miraculous bread in such abundance there were basketfuls left over. The parallels are pretty obvious. But less obviously, Jesus isn't only Moses in this story, he's also Elisha. If you know your Old Testament, you'll realize that some of the details of the story are taken from the story of Elisha in 2 Kings 4, who also took an army of men into the desert and fed them miraculously with a few loaves. So taking the two together, Mark is telling us that in recapitulating Moses Jesus fulfilled the Law, and in recapitulating Elisha he fulfilled the prophets. It's the same idea as when Mark shows us Moses and Elijah in person testifying to Jesus at the Transfiguration: we are being shown the dual testimony of the Law and the Prophecy to the true Messiah.

But still that's not all. In Mark (and Matthew) there is, strangely, an almost identical feeding miracle two chapters on, but with a different set of numbers of people, loaves, and fishes. And these numbers evidently matter, because in chapter 8 Mark shows Jesus questioning the disciples about them. 'Come on,' he says, 'Think. Five loaves for five thousand the first time round, seven for four thousand the second. Twelve basketfuls left over the first time, seven the second. See? Get it?' 'No,' they reply; and as so often in Mark, Jesus groans and starts telling them what deaf, blind, hard-hearted clothheads they are. So much for the simple, straightforward gospel! The disciples, alas, didn't have Nineham to explain to them what Mark presumably meant the reader to understand: that the symbolic numbers in the first miracle suggest a Jewish setting, and in the second the numbers suggest a Gentile one. In other words, the two stories are a sort of prefiguring of the two-stage preaching of the gospel: to the Jew first, then to the Gentile. The bread is evidently to be understood as the word of God: a symbolic interpretation of the manna in the Moses story which the rabbis had already drawn out of Deuteronomy 8:3, 'Man does not live by bread alone but by every word . . .'

But the bread is more than the word as preaching. Last of all there was an even more exciting hidden connection for a pious Anglo-Catholic young man. The prophets had foretold that in the last days God or the Messiah would himself come and feed his people, and heaven itself would be an eternal banquet of plenty. One rabbi contemporary with Jesus wrote that as the first Redeemer (Moses) fed his people in the desert, so would the last *eternally*. There is clearly a reference here to this eschatological meal. But isn't there also something familiar about those words, 'Jesus took the bread and blessed and broke and gave . . . '? They are the same actions as those of Jesus at the last supper in Mark 14. Even the fact that Mark mentions the grass was green is significant. Mark is the last writer in the world to give us incidental detail. What he is telling us is that the month is Abib, the month of green grass, the time of passover. The old passover meal which recalled God's redemptive act through Moses at the Exodus must also be recapitulated in a new meal recalling the redemptive work of God in Christ. So hooray! – we even have the Mass in here as well, yet another element in this extraordinary complex of allusions. The story looks

47

back to the old passover, and forward to the new celebration of the new passover in the Eucharist, and beyond that again to the eschatological banquet which the Eucharist itself foreshadows. (The eucharistic exegesis of the miracle was of course later made explicit in John's Gospel, chapter 6, and in early Christian iconography.)

I have written at some length about this, because I want to convey to you some of the excitement I found then and still find in the process of unlocking scrpture, 'breaking the word'. It is not simply an intellectual excitement, it is a spiritual excitement. For me discovering biblical criticism, so far from undermining or threatening my faith, brought the Bible back from the dead. It allowed me to engage with it, to get under its skin, and it in turn opened up to me mysterious depths and dimensions of meaning I had never imagined. I began to see why it might make sense to spend a lifetime studying it. I also realized, rather resentfully, how little my teachers and clergy apparently understood of what they purported to teach – or, if they did understand it, how bad they were at sharing it. In this connection I was delighted to find recently an essay by Christopher Evans entitled 'Should the New Testament be taught to Children?' His argument, which perfectly fits my own experience, is that scripture is taught at such a simplistic level in schools and churches that it is counterproductive. Sooner or later the questioning mind is almost bound to reject it, and may never discover any other approach. As he says,

> Perhaps the single largest counter factor to Christianity in our society . . . is the presence of so many young men and women who, as products of this system, are not only not ready to consider Christianity as a real option, but have been, perhaps permanently, immunized against it as something which has already been all heard before and seen through. It is not something to grow into, but something already grown out of.[2]

I get angry now when I attend certain Bible studies or missions in Oxford, and there is Mr Evans still peddling his disastrous nonsense, misrepresenting the Bible to generations of intelligent young people, who in later years will probably jettison the whole thing, or else painfully have to turn round and start again. Much of my ministry has had to consist of deprogramming students who have been screwed up and straitjacketed by just that sort of thing. But I get angry too with quite a few Miss Tomkinses in the academic and ecclesiastical world, who make it all too easy for the fundamentalists to claim that biblical criticism really means unbelief, or at best some cold shadow of the faith, which is really humanism with a religious veneer. I hate the fact that students flock to fundamentalism in droves; but I can hardly blame them, when the alternatives often seem so lacking in faith and fire.

How can we help people come to grips with the Bible and make it genuinely useful to them? Perhaps the first thing is to stop them being so killingly pious about it, and give them permission to start asking questions. A while ago I had the experience of sitting in a congregation on the seventh Sunday before Easter, when Numbers 15:32–6 came up in the Alternative Service Book. If you remember, Numbers 15:32–6 is the story of a poor Israelite man who went out to collect sticks to keep warm in the desert night, forgetting it was the sabbath, and got arrested by the guards. 'And so', the reader proclaimed, 'they dragged the man before Moses and Aaron, who said, "This man must be put to death. He must be stoned by all the community outside the camp." So they took him outside and they stoned him with stones as Moses and Aaron commanded, until he was dead. . . . *This is the word of the Lord*.' And we all replied: '*Thanks be to God*'! The most disturbing thing was that nobody turned a hair. Worse still, when the preacher referred to the passage in his sermon, he simply took it at face value. It didn't occur to him either to ask in what sense this barbarous little tale is supposed to be the word of God, or to question what on earth it is meant to tell us about God's nature.

At Mattins recently in our college chapel Psalm 109 was appointed for the day. So we all stood up and said (more or less):

O God, how I hate this man, your enemy and mine!
  Let him be found guilty when he is judged!

49

Let his days be few, and let even his prayer for help be counted
    as sin!
Let his children be fatherless, let his wife be made a widow,
And don't let anyone take pity on them either.
And now I come to think of it, curse his children's children,
And don't forget the sins of his parents too.

Glory be to the Father . . .

I am happy to say we couldn't finish it for laughing, which
is surely the only Christian reaction to such a piece of
unbridled malice. I worry about the churches where they
feel unable to laugh. But don't misunderstand me. It is
not that I would want to leave such texts out. Far from it.
I believe the ASB calendar is quite wrong to let us leave
them out. By definition Catholicism is about the *whole* faith
and the *whole* of scripture, with each part seen in the
context of the whole. What we need to do is to teach
people why such texts are there, and how to regard them.
It is not omission we need, but education – lots more
education. People desperately need teaching about how
the Bible grew, why parts of it are savage and parts sublime, and how to discriminate between them. They need
arming against the frightening advance of fundamentalism
in our own Church and in all the churches. They need
telling bluntly that the Bible, and still less any one text of
it, is *not* in an absolute sense 'the word of the Lord', only
Jesus is. He can speak to us through it, but he is not to
be identified with it; to vest unquestioning authority in
the written word instead of the living Word – to confuse
the letter and the spirit – is a particularly dangerous form
of idolatry.

As things are, most Christians are still approaching the
Bible as if it were a single book that dropped from heaven
in God's own handwriting. But of course it isn't one book,
it is eighty-four books written across the space of a thousand years and containing many traditions older than that.
In so far as it is inspired, it is not a unitary revelation
delivered by God, it is a kaleidoscope, a very jumbled and
messy kaleidoscope, consisting of many different authors'
insights into God at many different times and in many

different places. This naturally means that in the light of subsequent ideas some of the earlier ideas are seen to be wrong. From our point of view very many of them are wrong, but there is still a superstitious reluctance to say this, even among those who are not ideologically tied to a doctrine of inerrancy. Most Christians, it is true, have come to terms with the fact that the world was not literally made in seven days and that Adam and Eve are not our literal ancestors. But we have to be far clearer that parts of scripture are not only scientifically wrong or historically wrong, they are also morally and religiously wrong. The Bible's moral and religious ideas varied and developed as much as its ideas about the natural world. How could it be otherwise with such a multiplicity of different authors conflicting with and often correcting one another?

We have to teach people how, across this library of different books, and often within individual books or even within chapters and verses which have been re-edited at different stages, we move between polytheism and mono-theism, between the anthropomorphic God of the early Pentateuch to the sublime and universal Lord of deutero-Isaiah and Christ, between polygamy and monogamy, between animal sacrifice and repudiation of animal sacri-fice, between a tribal corporate morality and an individual-istic morality, between flat denial of an afterlife (in Job and Ecclesiastes) and firm assertions of it (in Daniel, parts of the Apocrypha and the New Testament). The differ-ences and contradictions of course are more marked within the Old Testament than the New because it covers so much more ground in terms of time, but there are plenty of differences and contradictions in the New Testa-ment too.

The biblical critic's job is to investigate these documents and ideas, to ask what are the relations between them, what are their source and setting and date in history; who is editing whom and why; what theological or sociological axes are grinding in the background; what are the literary forms which shape and condition what is written. These different avenues of investigation may have grand names – 'form criticism', 'redaction criticism', 'genre criticism' and so on – but they boil down to common-sense

51

questions which *must* be asked before we can place a biblical writer in context and extract his meaning. Otherwise (and my teachers' explanations of the Feeding of the Five Thousand are a case in point) the modern reader taking a text at face value is liable to miss or mistake its significance completely.

I realize of course that the critical approach can seem frightening and destructive, and I do not want to minimize the alarms and perplexities that serious bible study can entail. I said that for me it was exciting and inspiring to discover Mark's Gospel, and to find that a text like the Feeding of the Five Thousand is a sophisticated piece of literature, packed with nourishing allusions to dig out and relish. But of course one still finds oneself asking, Did it really happen? Was there some historical kernel behind the miracle story which Mark has elaborated? Or did he or someone before him simply compose it to be the vehicle of all those theological and symbolic references? One of my exegetical heroes is Austin Farrer, one of several admirable Anglo-Catholic practitioners of the literary-critical approach to the Bible, who specialized in investigating the patterns of allusion and typology which underlie gospel texts. But Farrer was strongly – and I think fairly – criticized for generally stopping short of the awkward historical questions which his own approach entailed. With the Feeding of the Five Thousand it might not seem to matter so much. But what about the stories of Jesus' birth and death and resurrection, since they too are packed with prophecy fulfilment and allegory and literary artifice? Could not they too be literary–theological creations woven out of nothing that actually happened, or at least out of very little? What about *all* the miracles, and the parables, and even straightforward ethical teaching like the Sermon on the Mount? Need they go back to Jesus at all? Some of the most interesting recent studies of the Synoptic Gospels by scholars in the succession of Farrer and Lightfoot not only dispense with Q, but argue that virtually everything in Matthew that is not in Luke is Matthew's own composition, and virtually everything in Luke that is not in the other two is Luke's. And they can point to parallel conventions of literary creation in Jewish theological writing to back up their view.

They are questions that have to be faced, and far be it from me to deny them or to claim easy solutions. But for what it's worth, I want to say for my own part that studying the New Testament critically has only confirmed my faith in the incarnation and resurrection of Jesus as historical fact. I also see no reason to doubt that the gospels taken together present a true picture of what he signifies, although that picture has been refracted through very different witnesses and at different levels of meaning, and *has* clearly undergone a lot of unhistorical literary elaboration in the process. If you are looking for the safest historical bottom line, I would say frankly that the place to look is probably not the gospels, but the letters of St Paul. That is not only because they were written earlier but, more importantly, because the letters are a factual genre of writing, which the gospels are not. When so much in gospel criticism seems so insecure, it is no small comfort that Paul in I Corinthians, an early letter, does speak in terms of an objective, historical resurrection to which there were eye-witnesses, without which our faith would be vain, and we should of all people be most to be pitied. That is language in our own register, something we can understand and rest on; and at the same time it provides external validation that whatever elaboration and interpretation they contain, the gospels are grounded in history, and are elaborating and interpreting something vast that really did happen. So even if, as with the Feeding of the Five Thousand, we must accept the possibility that a particular gospel story may not go back to Jesus, but has been created by his followers in the tradition as part of their interpretation of him, I do not personally find that a cause for nervous failure.

It ought to be said too that the critical method itself has its limitations. We have to try and enter into a biblical writer's meaning, but of course we are separated by huge differences of time and culture (Nineham himself emphasized, and perhaps over-emphasized, this in his book *The Use and Abuse of the Bible*). We can never enter entirely into someone else's past; and some recent critics, especially

those influenced by structuralism, take the very pessimistic view that we can never really understand what a
biblical writer meant, and so doubt the usefulness of standard critical methods altogether. Everything, they say, is
culture-specific and time-specific; there are no data or
'facts' which exist independently of the text in front of us.
Besides that, we too have our own point of view and our
own prejudices which, try as we might, we cannot help
reading into the text. All of which is true, of course; but
it can also be overstated. After all, it would be equally
true to say we can never in any full and objective sense
'know' any other person we encounter, even *within* our
own time and culture. We cannot get inside their skin, we
cannot inhabit their mental world, we see them only as
they show themselves to us, and only according to the
limitations of our own perceptions and prejudices about
them. Nevertheless we do not usually get so depressed
about this that we abandon the whole attempt to com-
municate with others and become hermits. I agree we
should not underestimate the difficulties of understanding
a writer who is writing in a very different conceptual
framework. But simply because we cannot be identical
with them does not mean we cannot still trace lines of
compatibility and continuity with them. We may not hear
them directly in our own language, as it were; but we can
still ask the question, as Leonard Hodgson put it, 'What
must be the truth for us now if people who thought as
they did put it like that?'[3] That is the crucial question of
exegesis; and for all its limitations, the critical method can
still take us a long way towards finding the answer.

Biblical criticism and Catholic tradition

Point 4 of Affirming Catholicism's statement of aims reads:
'We affirm that Catholic tradition is not a static but a living
thing, rooted in the revelation of Jesus Christ and growing
in the experience of the Church.' Much of what we have
said and written so far in this movement has been about
understanding Catholic tradition in this evolutionary way,
and not as a closed body of received doctrine and practice.
What we are after is an intelligent traditionalism, one

which keeps faith and continuity with its Catholic inherit-
ance, but which rejects the reactionary view of tradition
which has misunderstood tradition's own true nature.
When T.S. Eliot wrote 'Christianity is always adapting
itself into something which can be believed,' he wasn't
being cynical. He was merely stating a fact about the way
Christianity always has been, and has to be, in order to
be a living faith in every generation.

But much of what we have to say about tradition has
to be said about scripture too. As I have been reminding
you, scripture, like tradition, does not consist of unequivocal data, but is itself the product of centuries of continual
evolution and adaptation. Just as tradition is not something which we simply 'possess' from the past but something which we are part of and grow with, so scripture is
not a unitary body of material which stands over against
us, but something we constantly have to engage with and
reinterpret to our situation now.

It is perhaps not surprising that unaffirming Catholicism
tends to take the same static view of scripture that it takes
of tradition. To some extent this has always been a danger.
A hundred years ago hard-line Anglo-Catholics bitterly
criticized Charles Gore for tentatively accepting, in *Lux
Mundi*, that the Pentateuch was written not by Moses but
by J, E, D and P. A hundred years on I wonder how much
has changed. In the last few weeks the new International
Conference of Traditionalist Bishops has been bewailing
what it calls 'departures from scripture' in matters such
as the ordination of women and 'certain issues of personal
morality'. And last year there was a new wonder in
Christendom, when before the election of the new Archbishop of Canterbury representatives of the Church Union
joined with the Evangelical Church Society to demand that
the new man should 'uphold biblical authority without
equivocation'.

Could anyone who has seriously studied the Bible and
understood the nature of its contents claim to 'uphold
biblical authority without equivocation'? What would
'without equivocation' mean? Are all the bits of the Bible
supposed to be equally authoritative? Has the Church
Union really gone over to the doctrine of biblical

55

inerrancy? If the answer is, 'Er . . . well . . . no; we only mean authoritative in *some* parts or in *some* sense,' then we shall have to start thinking *which* parts, and in *what* sense, and *why* . . . and lo and behold, we have begun to equivocate! What else does 'equivocation' mean here, if not the thinking which somebody *must* do, if scripture is going to relate at all to the Church today?

For it is simply untrue to suggest that scripture gives 'unequivocal' answers to the kinds of question that now face the Church. It is misleading to say that the ordination of women to the priesthood is a 'departure from scripture'. Which bit of scripture? If it is Paul or deutero-Paul saying women must not hold authority over men, fine; but let us not forget that a female monarch or prime minister is equally a departure from that bit of scripture, so why are we not worried about that? And what about the other bits where Paul says women have to keep silent in Church, and wear veils, and learn from their husbands at home? We have departed from those too, thank the Lord – unless these bishops are wanting to bring back mantillas as well. And what about Galatians 3:28, where Paul implies that 'in Christ' distinctions of gender, as well as of race and class, are transcended? To pretend that there is an unequivocal Pauline ruling on this issue simply will not do.

Then there are these mysterious 'issues of personal morality' – meaning sex, of course, and in particular homosexuality. (As with certain politicians, the word 'morality' in these slogans never includes matters of wealth or justice or truth, only sex.) All right, but if they mean homosexuality, what is the biblical view? You can brandish Paul again, of course, but what does Paul understand by the words we translate as 'homosexual'? In Paul's society 'homosexuality' meant in practice pederasty or prostitution, which none of us wishes to defend. Furthermore Paul makes clear (in Romans I) his belief that those who engage in homosexual acts are really heterosexual, but have wilfully and perversely 'exchanged' their sexuality through conforming to a pagan culture. We know now this is not true. (Who in this society – still less in this Church – would be so idiotic as to *choose* homosexuality?)

What Paul says simply does not relate to the current issue. To ignore the context and use his words to condemn committed, Christian relationships between two adult women or men is exegetically as well as humanly indefensible.

What these formulaic appeals to biblical authority amount to is a demand that we stop thinking, bolster our prejudices and preserve the *status quo*. Certainly scripture can help us find the answer to our present perplexities; but only by understanding it as a whole, by weighing individual texts and teachings in the context of the whole, and so trying to discriminate between timeless principles and time-conditioned dogmas. Slogans which clamour for 'scripture and tradition' or condemn 'capitulation to the spirit of the age' make fine rhetoric, but the appeal is most often from ignorance to ignorance: ignorance above all of the adaptive nature of scripture itself, as being itself the record of continuous readjustment of theological teachings to changing historical and social conditions.

All right, you may say, but there must still be limits on this kind of interpretation. In particular, what makes an exegesis of scripture a Catholic one? If both scripture and tradition are evolutionary and adaptive by nature, how does the one relate to the other, and who sets the boundaries on interpretation and change?

In the bad old days of course the answer was easy, at least for Roman Catholics. There was no question but that the interpretation of scripture was strictly subordinate to tradition, 'tradition' meaning the teaching of the Church as currently formulated. This meant that not only the practical results of exegesis in terms of doctrine, but also the conduct and scope of exegesis itself were strictly limited by the magisterium. Until the 1950s it was binding on Roman Catholic scholars to teach, for instance, the single authorship of Isaiah, the priority of Matthew's Gospel, and the Pauline authorship of Hebrews and the Pastoral Epistles. Nor could they doubt, at least in print, that our Lady sang every literal word of the Magnificat – St Luke, presumably, having hidden behind a pillar! There was the bad old Catholic slogan, 'The Church to teach, the Bible to prove' – rather as if the Bible itself were no more than a quarry of knock-down texts with which to confound Protestants. (Ironically, you're less likely to hear that preached nowadays from Roman pulpits than from Anglo-Catholic ones).

The Roman reversal began in 1955, when Pius XII freed Catholic scholars from such restrictions, and promoted a considerable flowering of biblical scholarship, especially in France, which produced the first great Catholic Bible scholars of the century, such as De Vaux, Cerfaux and Lyonnet. But the spectacular change came with the Second Vatican Council, in its 'Dogmatic Constitution on Divine Revelation' (*Verbum Dei*), and in particular chapter 3 on the interpretation of scripture. This defines the aim of exegesis as discovering the original meaning of the scriptural authors in their own context, and it effectively legitimates all the methods of critical scholarship, though not of course any doctrinal conclusions to be drawn from them. The crucial passage says,

> In determining the intentions of the sacred writers attention must be paid *inter alia* to literary forms, for the fact is that truth is differently presented and expressed in the various types of theological writing, in prophetic and poetical texts, and in other forms of literary expression. Hence the exegete must look for that meaning which the sacred writer, in a determined situation and given the circumstances of his time and culture, intended to express and did in fact express, through the medium of a contemporary literary form. Rightly to understand what the sacred author wanted to affirm in his work, due attention must be paid both to the customary and characteristic patterns of perception, speech and narrative which prevailed at the age of the sacred writer, and to the conventions which the people of his time followed in their dealings with one another.[4]

When one remembers that literary form and convention must include, for example, the creation of myths and legends, the introduction of the miraculous, pseudonymous authorship, wholesale edition and alteration of sacred texts by subsequent authors, the editing and expansion of prior writings into new ones (like Matthew or Luke's use of Mark), then one begins to realize the remarkable scope this document affords – and the reason why conservative

Roman Catholics have been fighting it ever since. But there it stands, and the result of this new freedom to think has been an explosion of Catholic biblical scholarship in the last thirty years, especially in America and Germany.

Probably its greatest representative today – and one of the most respected biblical scholars of any confession – is Fr Raymond Brown, a member of the Sulpician teaching order and Professor of Biblical Studies at Union Theological Seminary, New York. Brown has no hesitation in repudiating the old proof-text method of exegesis which traditionally purported to find ready-made Catholic doctrines in selected texts; he insists 'it is crucial that we be aware that the church interpretation of a passage and the literal (i.e. original) sense may be quite different'.[5] So, for example, he points out as readily as any Protestant scholar that the Catholic Church's present concepts of episcopate and priesthood can hardly be found ready made, as used to be claimed, in the references to bishops and presbyters in Acts and the Pastoral Letters, though they are certainly a development out of them. He will agree that the New Testament in fact witnesses to a multiplicity of forms of ministry in its own period, and that this ought to make Catholics less dismissive of other churches' forms of ministry than they have 'traditionally' been.[6] He will calmly state that whereas devotion to our Lady certainly shows its beginnings in the Gospels of Luke and John, it might well have been anathema to Paul and, even more probably, to Mark.[7] In his various writings on the infancy narratives he makes it quite clear that the stories of Jesus' birth told by Luke and Matthew cannot both be literal history and almost certainly neither of them is. In terms of genre they are comparable to Haggadic Midrash in rabbinic literature, a sort of theologically-motivated storytelling designed to show that Jesus fulfilled the prophecies and patterns of redemption found in the Old Testament.[8]

It is hardly surprising if at certain points the shoe perceptibly pinches. When he deals with the question of the virginal conception of Jesus, Brown weighs meticulously the evidence which other biblical scholars cite as proof that it is simply another creation of the legend. In the New Testament only Matthew and Luke testify to it

59

(though since he believes their accounts are independent, Brown can also see this as an argument in favour of historicity). There is the suspicious fact that the Hebrew of Isaiah 7:14, 'A young woman shall conceive and bear a son,' was translated in the Greek version as 'a virgin shall conceive and bear a son'; and it appears to have been this Greek version of the prophecy which Matthew was intending his story to fulfil. So possibly – though Brown emphasizes that there is no corroborating evidence – the Greek text had already generated an expectation that the Messiah would be virgin-born. There are also possible, if distant, models for the virgin-birth idea in pagan myth and in Philo. And if we dare to go on to ask what then might have been the historical truth if not the virginal conception, it is striking that in Mark, the earliest Gospel, Jesus is called the Son of Mary, not of Joseph; and there is evidence that to be called after one's mother in that society may have implied that you were illegitimate. Furthermore in John's Gospel (8:41) the Jews attack Jesus on the precise grounds that he was born illegitimate, an accusation which the evangelist leaves unquestioned and unrefuted.[9]

In covering this ground Brown does his best to defend the historicity of the virginal conception, but has to conclude that in the nature of the case, as a matter of exegesis, the question is unprovable either way. As he says, in discussing this kind of literature he is consistently careful to avoid dogmatic historical statements such as, 'The magi did not exist,' or, 'The magi did exist,' since both claims are ultimately unverifiable. Like most exegetes, he is happier to underline that what counted in the evangelist's mind was the theological function of this element in his composition, but he can hardly escape the tendency of this observation itself to cast doubt on historicity, especially where the miraculous is concerned. Nevertheless as a matter of defined doctrine, which for Brown is an area of ecclesial obedience, he declares himself ready to submit to the authority of the Church. So he says he accepts 'as a Catholic' the virginal conception and indeed the perpetual virginity of Mary; but he strives (in my view successfully) never to let his confessional allegiance affect his presentation of the evidence.[10]

Let me say that I do not think Brown lacks integrity. But there is an obvious tension here, and it is not surprising that he has come under harsh and repeated attacks, both from conservative Catholics who regard him as a dangerous subversive, and from more liberal colleagues who accuse him of dishonesty and press him to draw more radical conclusions from his own research. As a 'centrist' in these debates (to use his own term) Brown sees his own function within the Catholic Church as a sort of broker between scripture and tradition, equally opposed to a static revisionism on the one hand and on the other to a liberalism which is too careless of its Catholic roots. As a prophet of what he calls a 'nuanced view of development'[11] he describes the task of the Catholic biblical theologian as 'moving the Church', 'moving all Christians to think'[12] – trying to promote change and development *within* the tradition of the Church by recalling it to scripture, and opening up to the Church scripture's real nature, meaning and challenge. It is sometimes an uncomfortable and vulnerable vocation, but an indispensable one. As he puts it:

> Tension is not an improper relationship between what the scripture meant to its authors and what it has come to mean in the Church . . . The literal sense of scripture uncovered through historical–critical research may challenge the Church; and it is incumbent on scholars not to present that challenge hostilely but by way of invitation . . . Scripture would not be the word of God if it always confirmed Christians or the Church . . . Jesus is not heard if at times he is not reminding God's people that we are capable of transgressing God's commandment for the sake of our own traditions (Matt. 15:3). A Bible at times in tension with the Church can serve as the conscience of the Church reminding it that it is not yet what it should be.[13]

Brown's description of this relationship between scripture and tradition corresponds closely to the relationship between the two as also described by Vatican II in *The Dogmatic Constitution on Divine Revelation*: (ch. 2, para. 9):

> Sacred tradition and sacred scripture are bound closely together and communicate with one another. For both of them, flowing out from the same divine well-spring, come together to form a single entity and move towards the same goal.

What this posits is a balance, a symbiosis of tradition and scripture, which recognizes not only what I have called the evolutionary nature of both, but that the evolution itself comes from the intercommunication between them. The picture is organic and dynamic, one of constant growth and progress through mutual dialogue. It remains true of course, as Catholics have always been keen to point out, that the Bible is secondary to the Church, both in the sense that its contents were written for already existing Christian communities, and in the sense that the Church itself formally fixed its canon. For that reason the Catholic exegete is always likely to feel psychologically and spiritually more secure than the Protestant who is still clinging to *sola scriptura*. The novelty of Vatican II is that it also brings out strongly the reciprocal authority that scripture must have over the Church. The best image I can think of is that the canon is like a genetic matrix, or a cross-section through the stem of a growing plant. It represents only a limited period in the Church's early life, and it is marked, as the Church always is, by human bias and error, but nevertheless it is determinative, it contains patterns for the future within it, and continues to feed and form the living organism which has developed out of it.

Perhaps more relevantly for us, we are given a similar picture of the relationship between the Bible and tradition in the Agreed Statement on Authority in the Church issued by the joint Anglican-Roman Catholic International Commission (ARCIC). This describes scripture as 'the normative record of the authentic foundation of the faith . . . to [which] the Church refers its teaching and practice. Through these written words the authority of the Word of God is conveyed.' At the same time it recognizes that the exegesis of scripture is a matter of 'unravelling' its meaning from its own context and expressing it in current language and thought – discerning through the written words Christ the living Word whom it conveys. And like Vatican II, ARCIC agrees that interpretation in terms of doctrine and practice is ultimately a matter for the common faith of the Church and not merely the individual: 'By reference to this common faith each person tests the truth of his own belief.'[14]

The upshot of all this is that there is no such thing as Catholic exegesis, there is only the Catholic exegete. The methods of biblical research itself are universal and based on reason; any scholar who bases research on any other considerations is simply a bad scholar. What makes you a Catholic exegete is the context you work in and how you relate to it the Church. As Brown says, it is the vocation of Christian scholars, and *a fortiori* of Catholic scholars, to feed their particular insights into the common mind of the Church, and to promote the development of that common mind. He or she must try to do this with rigorous intellectual honesty, but also with a sense of responsibility and with a due humility. The maverick who is out to shock and sell books will not fit the picture.

Some months ago a rather eminent Anglican biblical scholar who was feeling alienated from his Anglo-Catholic background asked a group of us in Affirming Catholicism if he could still count as a Catholic and disbelieve the historicity of the virginal conception. At the personal level the answer is clearly yes. He cannot unthink his thoughts or deny the honest findings of his own research, nor can he simply be told to shut up about it. As a scholar he clearly has a duty to continue thinking and discussing his position with those who take a different view. He also has a duty not to present his view insensitively or sensationally or destructively (he would hardly be right to come straight out with it at the Christmas Midnight Mass). Going back to Hodgson's question, 'What must be the truth now if a biblical writer who thought in that way put it like that?', he has a further duty to try and convey fully and constructively what impelled Matthew and Luke to tell the story that way, and why it matters for us. He has to consider how his view relates to other areas of faith and doctrine, notably the incarnation and devotion to our Lady. (He may of course conclude that it is more helpful than harmful to both, but he then has a duty to explain why.) Above all, if he speaks or writes about it publicly he has to make it clear that this is his opinion, not the mind of the Church, though he has every right to hope that the Church will move towards including it, and to work to that end.

All this is surely part of the process of dialogue between tradition and scripture as Vatican II and ARCIC describe it. And of course it's nothing new. It is by the same process that the Church throughout its history has continually adjusted its position after it has been faced with new truths and new insights. It is undeniably a messy process, and for those who are urging change the time lag between insight and acceptance is agonizingly slow. Tensions and quarrels are unavoidable, but they are not signs of decay and imminent dissolution; they are signs of life. As long as disagreement is not allowed to become division, the pains of disagreement generally turn out to have been growing pains in the end.

One of the fruits of studying scripture is that it teaches you that things have never been different. Preaching on the feast of Saints Peter and Paul last Sunday I found myself recalling the row that the two of them had at Antioch about eating with Gentiles: Paul the radical fighting for freedom from the Law and ethnic inclusiveness; and Peter, the Rock, harking back to the Jerusalem Church, the old ways and the *status quo*.[15] It is remarkable – or it seems remarkable to me – that the tension between these two fundamentally opposed religious attitudes not only arises as a result of the earliest Christian witness, but is there right at the heart of that witness itself; so that across the epistles and gospels we are unavoidably seeing Jesus now through a more conservative pair of spectacles, now through a more radical pair. If the New Testament is the Church's genetic matrix, this kind of dialectic is locked into our genes, and it is silly to get despondent about it. Like the debate about the Gentiles in the first century or the debate about Genesis in the last, our current rows about women's ordination, homosexuality or the virginal conception will pass into obscurity, and our grandchildren will wonder how we can have been so foolish.

But by that time they will be busy with their own rows. The Spirit of Truth leads us *slowly* to the truth that makes us free. Or to quote the rather sharper observation of one anonymous commentator:

> Remember. The Church goes through four stages of response to any challenge to its tradition. First, we pretend the challenge isn't there. Then we argue vehemently against it. Then we admit exceptions and qualifications. Last of all, we insist that's what we *really* thought all along.

1 D.E. Nineham, *Saint Mark* (Penguin, 1963).
2 C.F. Evans, *Is 'Holy Scripture' Christian? and Other Questions* (SCM Press, 1971), pp. 46–7.
3 Quoted in D.E. Nineham, *The Use and Abuse of the Bible* (SPCK, 1978); see especially pp. 222 and 264.
4 *The Dogmatic Constitution on Divine Revelation (Dei Verbum)* 1965, ch. 3, para. 2.
5 Raymond Brown, *The Critical Meaning of the Bible* (Paulist Press, New York, 1981), p. 35; see also his *Biblical Exegesis and Church Doctrine* (Geoffrey Chapman, 1985) and *Biblical Reflections on Crises Facing the Church* (Darton, Longman and Todd, 1975).
6 Brown, *Critical Meaning*, pp. 35–6, 47–8, 96–106, 124–46.
7 Op. cit., pp. 42, 79–80; Brown, *Biblical Exegesis*, ch. 5; Brown, *Biblical Reflections*, ch. 5.
8 See Raymond Brown, *The Birth of the Messiah* (Geoffrey Chapman, 1977), especially Appendix VIII.
9 See Brown, *The Birth of the Messiah*, especially Appendices IV, V and pp. 122–64; also Raymond Brown, *The Virginal Conception and Bodily Resurrection of Jesus* (Paulist Press, New York, 1971), pp. 21–65.
10. See e.g. Brown, *Critical Meaning*, pp. 38–9, 60, 79–80; Brown, *Biblical Exegesis*, ch. 4; Raymond Brown, *101 Questions on the Bible* (Geoffrey Chapman, 1990), pp. 76–82.
11 See especially Brown, *Biblical Exegesis*, ch. 2.
12 Brown, *Critical Meaning*, chs. 4 and 5.
13 Ibid., pp. 41, 43–4.
14 ARCIC, *Final Report*, pp. 52–3 and Elucidations pp. 69–71.
15 Galatians 2.

4 What Sort of a Society Are We Envisaging Now?*

Alan Billings

Are there theological resources in the Anglican Catholic tradition which can contribute towards the renewal of the nation's social vision?

Let me begin by saying what I mean by social vision and why it needs renewing. Just as individuals need to have some sense of direction to their lives if they are to make choices and determine priorities, so a nation needs some overall vision by which it orders its collective life. To have a social vision is to be able to do two things. First, to be able to envisage how you can obtain those human goods which can only be obtained by individuals and groups working together; and second, given the scarcity of resources, to have an idea which of those social goods ought to have priority. Without social vision democratic politics will always be a matter of short-term responses to the most immediate issue or the most compelling vested interest. Behind all our politics lies the deeper and prior question: What sort of a society are we envisaging?

The erosion of social vision

If this were a sermon I would be tempted to reach for three texts. One would be for the nation: 'For the Lord God of hosts has a day of tumult and trampling and confusion in the valley of vision . . . ' (Isa. 22:5). One would be for the Church: 'And the word of the Lord was rare in those days; there was no frequent vision' (I Sam. 3:1). The third – a felicitous mistranslation in the Author-

*© Alan Billings 1991

ized Version – would remind us that: 'Where there is no vision the people perish' (Prov. 29:18).[1]

My text for the nation implies that we are passing through a period of confusion. That is true not only for this country at this particular moment; it is true more generally of all the western (and now eastern) European nations. To some extent we have lost our way.

In Britain we have seen the collapse of consensus around the post-war social vision of a welfare state. By the mid 1960s both those on the political left and, more particularly, those on the right were aware of how and to some extent why the reality of the welfare state was falling short of the vision (though each tended to highlight the shortcomings rather differently). The litany of failure is now well rehearsed: the creation of a culture of dependency; the bureaucratization of the social services and the subversion of their stated aims by that bureaucracy; the inability of governments to predict accurately the consequence of policies; the failure to eliminate poverty and achieve economic equality; the raising of welfare expectations divorced from considerations of wealth creation.

By the time of the 1979 general election the nation needed either a renewed social vision or a fresh one. In the event, the Conservative government of Margaret Thatcher sought to commend a different vision of society which owed more to the values of the new, radical Right than to old-style Conservatism of the Macmillan–Heath variety. There was to be a move away from the more corporatist state, an emphasis on the freedom of the individual, a more market-orientated economy and a deep suspicion of politics as a means of distributing national resources. The present confusion in this country is the result of the sudden rejection of Margaret Thatcher as Conservative leader. How far is that also a rejection of that radical alternative vision by the party she so recently led?

But there is a wider, longer-term confusion brought about by the collapse and discrediting of socialist régimes in eastern Europe and the ideology of socialism there and elsewhere. If neither 'Thatcherism' nor socialism is to provide the vision for new political projects, then what is? There is confusion in the valley of vision.

There must also be anxiety. If it is the case that across the whole of Europe socialist theory and practice is being abandoned and capitalism has triumphed, we need to register that what has triumphed is not the *laissez-faire* capitalism of the early nineteenth century. In a recent article Professor David Marquand notes how for the past century and more free-market capitalism has been significantly modified and held in check by the omnipresent moral and political challenge of socialism. 'Capitalism put its house in order because socialism put it on its mettle.' Marquand therefore asks, 'Now that the challengers are silenced what happens to the challenged?' He points out that there was nothing inevitable about this historic compromise of a reformed welfare capitalism and it may be a very fragile creation easily destroyed, especially where the lessons of history are not learnt. 'Left to itself, the capitalist free market still despoils the environment, both social and natural, and rewards the strong while punishing the weak.' 'It is', he also writes, 'a marvellous servant but a disastrous master.'

He identifies a paradox: socialism as an economic theory or a science of society or a vehicle for working-class aspirations or a secular religion is probably dead. Yet socialism as an ethic and an insight has come to underpin the very capitalism which socialism as an ideology sought to destroy – though in fact could only reform. What he refers to here is the socialist ethic of 'fraternity' and 'co-operation' (he does not believe that 'classical socialism' was much concerned with 'equality') and 'the insight that all societies, even capitalist ones, depend upon communities; and that community ties are public goods, which the competitive free-market economy cannot supply but can destroy'. A society based on 'the acquisitive individualism of market economics' would 'break the mainspring of mutual trust on which all societies depend'. The over-riding question for the post-socialist era, therefore, is whether 'insight and ethic can be brought together in a new project with some purchase on social reality'.[2]

I am not as convinced as Marquand about the death of

socialism nor am I persuaded that equality was not an important part of the socialist ethic; but I would otherwise broadly share his view. How then are we to think about renewing social vision? I would want to say that we need to recognize that capitalism is not itself an ideology with a social vision: it is only a mechanism, a means to an end. It is true that the economics of capitalism have often been developed into a deterministic ideology. It is also true that for markets to work certain 'properties' have to be encouraged – economic self-interest, profit, a level of inequality, etc. – which unrestrained by morality or regulation could have undesirable consequences for society as a whole. But markets are only a means to an end, and the end has to be provided by people's social vision.

If we need a renewed social vision embracing something like the socialist ethic and insight and performing a similar function – and I believe we do – is there a Christian contribution to be made and, more particularly, are there theological resources in the Catholic tradition of the Church of England which might be drawn upon? This is where I might turn to the text for the Church: 'The word of the Lord was rare in those days; there was no frequent vision.'

The vision is not frequent for the Church because for at least two decades the social ethics of the ecumenical movement and of churches influenced by liberation theology have been largely concerned with denouncing capitalism and looking to some form of socialism as an alternative way forward. The collapse of socialism and communism must now plunge these approaches into profound crisis. Liberationist-socialist political projects now look like a cruel illusion.

For Anglican Catholics the vision is not frequent partly for similar reasons in that a good deal of Catholic social theology this century has been anti-capitalist, but also because we have rather lost sight of the social tradition of Anglican Catholicism altogether. So let us briefly remind ourselves of that tradition and then ask whether there is anything in it which can resource our reflections on this new situation. I will then return to the issues raised by Professor Marquand.

Social Catholicism in the nineteenth century

The Catholic movement in the Church of England has passed through a number of phases and exhibited varying responses towards social issues. The social concerns and social theology which we associate with later generations of Anglican Catholics developed slowly over a period of years.

The Tractarians (1833–1845) were not particularly interested in social issues at all. In important respects their theology was set in an Evangelical frame: they were primarily concerned with sin, the soul, its redemption and God. They differed from the Evangelicals in emphasizing the sacraments as the means of redemption; but their concern remained largely the redemption of the individual human soul not the redemption of the world as a whole. As for social involvement, Keble distrusted anything which was not directly religious and this distrust was shared by other Tractarians. It was one reason for Von Hügel declaring the movement 'not really Catholic'.[3]

Newman said in old age that he had 'never considered social questions in their relation to faith, and had always looked upon the poor as objects for compassion and benevolence';[4] though he also wrote that the Church was 'framed for the express purpose of interfering, or (as irreligious men will say) meddling with the world'. It was not Newman, however, but Manning whose conversations with Pope Leo XIII inspired the Roman Catholic Church's great social encyclical on industrial society *Rerum Novarum* in 1891. The Tractarians were concerned with matters more narrowly theological, reaching back to the Fathers for their authority and illumination. Their central concern was the spiritual autonomy and authority of the Church of England. This completely absorbed them. For this reason, although he had once been associated with them, F.D. Maurice came to attack them, especially when legal controversies over increasing ritualism began to deflect their attention away from what Thomas Carlyle called the 'condition of England question'.

But there were emphases in Tractarian thinking which could be developed into a more social theology. The tendency of Evangelicalism, with its emphasis on personal salvation, was individualistic. The tendency of the Oxford Movement was towards the social: it emphasized the sacraments and the Church; it moved away from the Atonement as the central Christian doctrine to that of the Incarnation; and it rejected the Evangelical tendency to identify 'the world' with particular 'persons or pleasures or occupations'.[5] 'The world' was the whole world considered in its fallen state. It was this whole world that Christ came to redeem. But there was no systematic theological approach to social issues by way of analysis, prescription and action.

The Tractarians had an essentially emotional response to the conditions of nineteenth-century industrial and urban Britain: shock at the wretchedness of the poor and anger at the unrestrained pursuit of luxury on the part of the wealthy. Pusey was appalled at 'our miles of misery in our large towns'; Newman lamented the slavery to the world which prosperity fostered.[6] This slavery he defined as 'that low ambition which sets everyone on the lookout to succeed, and to rise in life, to amass money, to gain power, to depress his rivals . . . this most fearfully earthly and grovelling spirit is likely, alas! to extend itself more and more among our countrymen – an intense, sleepless, restless, never wearied, never satisfied pursuit of Mammon in one shape or another, to the exclusion of all deep, all holy, all calm, all reverent thoughts.'[7]

A major weakness of the Tractarians, which they shared with the Church more generally, was their ignorance of the real conditions of the poor and their lack of contact with working-class people and their organizations. To some extent this was remedied by the next phase of the movement – the parochial revival after 1845. Pusey urged the Church to send its clergy wherever the need was greatest: to the cities; but also 'to penetrate our mines, to emigrate with our emigrants, to shift with our shifting population' and, significantly, 'to grapple with our manufacturing system as the Apostles did with the slave-system of the Ancient world'.[8]

By this time the Catholic revival had been influenced by the thinking of Maurice and the Christian Socialists. In

Maurice's anthropology people were made in God's image for co-operation not competition, while the controlling principle in his theology was the concept of the Kingdom of God. 'The Kingdom of Heaven is to me the great practical existing reality which is to renew the earth and make it a habitation for blessed spirits instead of for demons.'[9] As a result he was a critic of the capitalist system and the 'properties' it encouraged and required – competition, self-interest, and inequality. This antipathy towards the market economy has coloured Christian social thinking ever since.

In the second half of the century the self-sacrificial ministries of the slum priests were one of the more remarkable features of the Victorian Church. But while some were 'as interested in the direction of sewers as of souls', many could not see the connection. Their priorities remained evangelical. Father Lowder at St George's Mission said that the primary object of ministry was to save souls and philanthropic work tended to secularize both priest and people. The main thrust of his work and that of most slum priests was to teach the Catholic faith and secure intense devotion to the person of our Lord in the sacrament of the altar. However, even where priests were most nervous about social action they were still heavily involved in it. The theology of this was rarely explored. The work was undertaken in the light of the parable of the Great Assize: in doing this for the poor they did it for him.

The third phase of Anglican Catholicism went far beyond works of charity and social welfare in developing the Church's social mission. As the century moved towards its close and then in the years leading up to the First World War, socialist ideas and a more corporatist approach to social questions gained ground in Catholic circles – as they had been gaining ground more generally.

A large number of organizations embracing Catholicism and socialism sprang up for a while under F. Lewis Donaldson's slogan 'Christianity is the religion of which socialism is the practice.' The more radical tradition began with Stewart Headlam's Guild of St Matthew (GSM), founded in 1877, which brought together Maurice's incarnational theology, sacramentalism and a more full-blooded socialism. From this we can trace a line of radical, often socialist, organizations which came and went with the years. They have been prophetic but largely peripheral to the life of the Church – though we should remember Conrad Noel's judgement that the existence of small, radical groups may prevent living orthodoxy from being stifled by dull conventionality.

Much larger in membership and representing a more respectable and genteel approach was the Christian Social Union (CSU) which grew out of the 'Holy Party', a liberal Catholic group formed in Oxford in 1875 around Charles Gore, B.F. Westcott and Henry Scott Holland. The GSM witheringly described their approach to social issues as, 'Here's a glaring evil, let's read a paper about it.' It is true that the socialism of the CSU was hardly more than an opposition to individualism and an advocacy of co-operation; members had little idea of the scale of what was needed by way of state action if wealth were to be redistributed or structures of power changed. Henry Major believed that the CSU did transform the Church of England: 'She who had been aptly described as the Conservative Party at prayer, became . . . at least in the persons of her Anglo-Catholic clergy, the Socialist Party at Mass.'[10] This is almost certainly a case of being generous with the truth. However, their mildly reformist socialism influenced William Temple and became the dominant force in English social theology until the Second World War, contributing to the vision of a welfare state – a term which Temple may have coined. In that sense we can probably claim that they achieved at least as much for the working classes as the more radical groups.

The 'Holy Party' also made a considerable impact on the Church of England by publishing in 1889 (the year that the CSU was founded) the volume of essays *Lux Mundi: A Series of Studies in the Religion of the Incarnation*. This was a turning point for the Catholic movement, for it spoke of the need for Christian thought to take into account advances in knowledge and changing circumstances. The essays emphasize 'Catholic' themes which became more generally influential in the Church: the incarnation is regarded as the basis of doctrine; the Christian ethic is seen as a social ethic with the Kingdom of God as its controlling idea; matter can be the vehicle of grace. After *Lux Mundi* and Gore's Bampton Lectures of 1891, Catholic social theology is decidedly 'incarnational': Christ came to redeem the whole world of matter and nothing less than the redemption of the whole world should be the concern of Catholics. It is also increasingly critical of capitalism and looks towards collectivist solutions to society's problems.

Social Catholicism in the twentieth century

We need at this point to remind ourselves how different this developing social Catholicism of the late nineteenth and early twentieth centuries was from the dominant movement in European Protestanism. Adolf von Harnack described the prevailing Protestantism as 'religious individualism' and 'subjectivism'. In a series of lectures in 1900 he explained this in relation to the preaching of Jesus on the parables:

> Anyone who wants to know what the kingdom of God and the coming of the kingdom mean in Jesus' preaching must read and meditate on the parables . . . The kingdom of God comes by coming to individuals, making entrance into their souls, and being grasped by them. The kingdom of God is indeed God's rule – but it is the rule of a holy God in individual hearts . . . It is not a matter of angels and devils, nor of principalities and powers, but of God and the soul, of the soul and its God.

And again: ' . . . it is the individual who is redeemed, not the people or the state'.[11]

The period between the two world wars marked the high point of the Catholic movement in the Church of England – though we should not forget that the movement's influence has been throughout the Anglican communion, inspiring in more recent years such courageous ministries as those of Trevor Huddleston and Desmond Tutu. The 1920s and 1930s saw the Anglo-Catholic congresses, huge rallies, which thrilled to the sermons and addresses of men such as Frank Weston, Bishop of Zanzibar. His often quoted address to the congress of 1923 gives something of the flavour of the Catholic approach to Christianity and social affairs at that time. He said:

> You cannot claim to worship Jesus in the Tabernacle, if you do not pity Jesus in the slum . . . It is folly – it is madness – to suppose that you can worship Jesus in the Sacraments and Jesus on the throne of glory, when you are sweating him in the souls and bodies of his children.[12]

This type of confident and inspirational speaking deeply moved the hundreds of people who heard it and had the undoubted effect of propelling many people towards the political cause of socialism.

In 1922 a volume of essays was published called *The Return of Christendom*. It was introduced by Charles Gore and had an epilogue by G.K. Chesterton, who was still an Anglican at that time. The heart of the book was not, as the title might suggest, an idealization of medievalism – though Catholics did often look back to the medieval period – but the articulation of the conviction that the 'regulative principle' in Christian social concern should be the idea of the Kingdom of God rather than any moral idealism of the times. The Church must not be confused or equated with the Kingdom but it was the herald of the Kingdom.

The group associated with the book – soon to become the Christendom Group – initiated Anglo-Catholic Summer Schools of Sociology which continued into the post-war period. The motivating conviction here was that if society were to flourish it had to be organized according to Catholic design and Catholic design followed from Catholic doctrine. That doctrine, with the incarnation and the sacraments at the centre, implied that

> the social life of man is not purely material; it is the interaction of spiritual and material relationships, and as such is truly destined for the reign of Christ, who in the central mystery of Catholic worship has pierced through even the semi-spiritual, semi-material fact of human society, to the mere matter of the world and 'assumed' it unto Himself.

The slogan now became 'Christianity is the religion of

which Christianity is the practice', and there was a distancing from the trade union and labour movement.[13]

Sympathetic to the position of the Christendom Group was Michael Ramsey who published in 1936 an influential book, *The Gospel and the Catholic Church*. Ramsey had a high doctrine of the Church, seeing it as an extension of the incarnation – and the passion – of Christ, and as such part of the gospel as well as the means by which the gospel was communicated. However, the Church was always subject to scripture: 'Catholicism always stands before the church door at Wittenberg to read the truth by which she is created and by which also she is judged.'[14] It is important to mention this because Anglican Catholicism has had to guard itself against both liberals without and ritualists within who for different reasons have not given to scripture the centrality which it historically has had within the Church of England. In his book Ramsey stressed the social nature of the Church and pointed the way to seeing the Church as the organism through which society will be transformed. As a result he was a fierce critic of individualism: it had no place in Christianity.

As war approached the Christendom Group became less optimistic about human nature and possibility. They were influenced by the writings of Christopher Dawson and Reinhold Niebuhr. During the war the doctrine of original sin became a more prominent feature of Christian anthropology and the radicalism of earlier social Catholicism began to wane.

Since the Second World War there has been a decline of Anglican Catholicism in part because its causes have succeeded: the Church of England is more sacramental than it was and many of Catholicism's social concerns were met with the creation of the welfare state and growing post-war affluence.[15] Indeed if we were to ask, 'What sort of a society did Anglican Catholics envisage for Britain after the war?' it would bear a strong resemblance to what the post-war Labour government in fact created: a welfare state in which key sectors of British industry were taken into public ownership. It was a strongly collectivist social vision.

This now presents social Catholicism with a major problem which is insufficiently acknowledged. The principal social issue for Anglican Catholics until the welfare state was the question of poverty. There is still poverty, of course; but it is not what it was. We live now in a society of increased and increasing, though uneasy, affluence. The working class is shrinking – though we have created a smaller and seemingly permanent underclass. We find all this hard to assimilate. Catholic social concern – as with Christian social concern more generally – is much more at home with the classic problems of poverty and lack of opportunity than the new problems of affluence and freedom. As a consequence we often have little to say about the very society in which we are called to minister: our social concerns are frequently not those of most people and we are not addressing important contemporary issues. It is my contention that social Catholicism is in urgent need of re-examination and reformulation. In particular, its historic rejection of the market economy, its Maurician suspicion of 'individualism' and its espousal of collectivist solutions mean that it risks being irrelevant to a society which has accepted a greater role for markets, is concerned about the freedom of the individual and is suspicious of corporatism – while being uneasy about the consequences of this, as Professor Marquand's concerns illustrate.

The Catholic approach to social issues

If this is the case, is there anything in this brief sketch of Anglican Catholic social concern which is distinctive of Catholics which might help us to see what contribution we might make towards renewing social vision today?

If we look at the period when the Catholic movement was at its height in the inter-war years, two things may be noticed which, with qualification, can help us now. First, there is the Catholic method of approach to social questions and second there are particular doctrinal emphases.

The Catholic method of approach to social questions was to begin with traditional Christian doctrine. 'Christian social teaching', wrote D.G. Peck in 1940, 'should be grounded on elementary fundamental Christian dogma.'[16] How one lived in community or organized industry could be deduced *a priori* from Christian doctrine. (An example of the latter would be the 'Signposts' series of paperbacks published during the Second World War. Peck's *Catholic Design for Society* began with fundamental Christian beliefs – about the nature of God, his relationship to and purposes for the world; the nature and destiny of people; the Church and sacraments – which were then applied to such social institutions as the family and industry.) As far as it goes this approach has more to commend it than the tendency of liberal Christianity to derive social and political positions from the general intellectual climate of the time and then look to support them from scripture and doctrine. But beginning with doctrine is only the first step: Catholic social thinking also needs to be thoroughly grounded in social reality. If Catholics are to engage in serious theological reflection on social issues they need to develop on the one hand a coherent theological frame (beliefs about God and his relationship to the world) which they bring to bear on social questions; and on the other, a thorough understanding of the social situation they are addressing. Social theology emerges from the interaction which takes place as we bring together and reflect upon the theological frame and the analysis of a social situation. The weakness of so much Catholic social theology in the past has been its lack of any thorough-going understanding of social situations. This method of approach, however, is not distinctive of Catholics: there has been a considerable convergence amongst Christian people in recent years about how to reflect on social issues and a recognition of the interactive nature of social theology.

In the second place we notice the consequences of particular Catholic emphases in doctrine – the Incarnation, the Mass, the Church, the Kingdom of God.

Evangelical theologies tend to emphasize the transcendence of God and see redemption in terms of rescuing individual souls from this fallen world. They will often take a pessimistic view of human nature and possibility. Consequently, the atonement and the cross are central in the Evangelical theological frame and the Kingdom of God is often conceived as wholly future if not beyond the world of space-time altogether. Catholic theology tends to be immanental and corporate and takes a more optimistic view of human nature. Percy Widdrington said in 1945 of his generation of Catholic priests that 'belief in the Incarnation and the Mass constituted our theological basis'.[17] God in Christ took human flesh and entered the world he had made to reclaim flesh and matter for himself. God became what we are in order to raise us up and make us what he is. In the mass, material things are taken and transformed; but what is transformed is not just bread but bread as symbol of the whole life of the world.

In other words, where theology is incarnational and sacramental, it leads to a high view of human nature and possibility, a valuing of the world and social involvement. The Kingdom of God is not only eschatological event but can be experienced as foretaste in the eucharistic community and to some extent incarnated in the life of the wider society. But where the incarnation is less central it can result in a devaluing of humanity and a withdrawal from the world. Such a pessimistic and low view of humanity pervades western Christianity. It is certainly one of the starting points for the theological reflections of C.S. Lewis who wrote in 1943: 'Christ takes it for granted that men are bad. The real test of being in the presence of God is that you either forget about yourself or see yourself as a small dirty object.'[18]

There are, however, dangers in the Catholic emphasis: it can lead to a blandness and complacency in the face of injustice and a facile optimism which overlooks the sheer depth of evil of which human beings are capable. Catholics do well to remember that Christ can also be 'against culture'. (Much of this rather bland incarnationalism was swept away by the rise of totalitarianism. But when times are easier it reappears.)

Just before the Second World War, perhaps as a result of the influence of Karl Barth, the doctrine of the Trinity came to exercise a more central role in Catholic thinking. Conrad Noel, vicar of Thaxted and founder of the strongly socialist Catholic Crusade, began a book in 1939 with a chapter entitled, 'The Blessed Trinity as the Basis of a New

World Order'. Over the past couple of decades Fr Ken Leech has written extensively about the Trinity as the theological basis for Christian social action. The Trinity speaks of a God who is 'social' and 'involved'; therefore a purely personal gospel or an uninvolved Christianity is not possible.[19] I believe that reflection on the Trinity is important at this time for other reasons too – and to these I now turn.

Resourcing social vision today

If part of the social task of the Church is to contribute towards the renewal of the nation's social vision, what is there in the Catholic tradition that can resource our thinking today? I have already suggested that we need to reformulate Catholic social vision in the light of changing circumstances, and we do that by that same combination of method of approach and particular doctrinal emphases which we have just been considering.

As far as method of approach is concerned we need to develop both the theological frame and our understanding of the current situation. That frame consists of beliefs about the divine economy (the way God relates to his world) and anthropology (the nature and destiny of human beings). Our understanding of the contemporary situation requires us to draw upon secular disciplines and sources of information. But the secular disciplines, such as sociology and economics, will be subject to scrutiny from the standpoint of the theological frame (which will in turn take secular knowledge into consideration) since no account of a secular situation is ever value free. (Liberation theologians who use Marxist social analysis can sometimes be quite uncritical at this point.) Before we can make any contribution we need to work for a genuinely interactive social theology.

Let me now return to the issues I raised earlier when quoting from Professor Marquand. What sort of a society are we now envisaging? Herein lies the dilemma.

It is now almost universally accepted that the sort of society we envisage is one in which there is much greater use of markets as the means of distributing resources and the role of the state is greatly reduced. After experiences in both the East and West there is a widely accepted view that market forces deliver goods and services more efficiently than centrally planned economies. The more corporatist states with their failed economies have been rejected. At the same time we have rejected the ideologies associated with corporatism – namely socialism in its various forms. But in the West socialism provided the moral context of capitalism so that the rejection of socialism may also mean the dissolving of that moral context – the sense of mutual obligation, the sense of interdependence, the sense of 'fraternity' and 'community'. In addition, as part of the rejection of corporatism, we have also come to stress the individual. Much of the appeal of Thatcherite politics lay in the idea of setting the individual free. The more corporate dimension is dissolved, or at least considerably diminished: 'There is no such thing as society, only individual men and women and their families.' The general direction of this is away from traditional social Catholicism which in the past has taken a more collectivist approach and attacked 'individualism'.

To put the matter rather bluntly, therefore, the question for Catholics now is this: what contribution can the Catholic tradition make towards a social vision in which the market economy can serve the individual without losing sight of fraternity and community? This is the crucial issue for social theology today.

There are two areas where I believe Catholic doctrine and practice can offer insight – though social theology is probably best resourced ecumenically. The first is concerned with how we understand what it is to be a person; the second follows from it and is concerned with persons-in-community.

(1) Reflections on the concept of the person
We need to be clear ourselves and then help others to be clear about the difference between the concept of the 'individual' and the concept of the 'person', for at present they are used interchangeably and not distinguished. Then we shall be able to see what enables 'persons' to

flourish and why 'individualism' is not at all the same thing but actually threatens that.

The concept of the autonomous, isolated individual, the rational thinking being – *cogito ergo sum* – is probably a consequence of the Enlightenment. It is certainly 'pervasive in the western tradition'. But it is based on a lie – the lie that you ever were or could be independent – as if society did not originally nurture and even now sustains people. But it is a lie which entrepreneurial societies will encourage. Against this we need to recover the concept of the person as we have it in the doctrine of the Trinity by reaching back, as the Tractarians would have done, to the theology of the Fathers. Here I have found particularly helpful the discussion of the Trinity in the theology of the Cappadocian fathers as set out in a British Council of Churches report, *The Forgotten Trinity*.[20]

In that theology the conception of the person is not individualistic but rather supports a social and communitarian understanding of human being. The Fathers were concerned with the notion of what it was 'to be', and saw in the doctrine of the Trinity – in the words of Basil of Caesarea – 'a new and paradoxical conception of united separation and separated unity'. The key is to understand the being of God as a 'relational unity': 'It consists in the fact that it is a communion, a being in which the persons give to and receive from each other what they are.' The report goes on:

> When such a conception is used to throw light on created personhood, it will be seen to generate neither an individualist nor a collectivist conception of the person. Particularity is at the heart of what is given and received, but, rather than being the denial of social relations, it is in fact its basis, because reciprocity and relationship are present from the outset and not tacked on as extra . . . To be a person on this account is to be what one gives to and receives from the other persons with whom one is in relation.[21]

This understanding of what it is to be a person also preserves the freedom of each person – an important point to make in the context of contemporary concerns about the freedom of the individual, which is an issue of paramount concern both to the radical Right in this country (who in this respect probably reflect the views of the majority) and to those who are shaking off the shackles of communism. To be a person is to be what one freely gives to and receives from those persons with whom one is in relation.

The issue of what it is to be a person and what sort of society sustains personal values is a concern of all, not just Christians. This is therefore an area where Christian reflection may have a contribution to make which the rest of society might actually want to hear. Our insight derives from our reflection on the nature of personhood in the Holy Trinity. The uniqueness, particularity and freedom of each person is preserved, but not in a way which is opposed to social relationships because the being of each particular person is precisely the result of relating to other persons.

This leads directly to the second area where we might make a contribution – a contribution, however, in deed as well as word.

(2) The ethic of fraternity

Professor Marquand's principal fear was that we should lose in our society any feeling for fraternity or community. A Catholic contribution towards the renewal of social vision can emerge both from reflection on the concept of the Church as the body of Christ and also from being the church in a particular place. Christians cannot tell people how to live together fraternally or in community unless they practise it in their local churches. The world will be persuaded by good news but not good advice.

Catholics have always been clear that the Church is a visible community founded by Jesus Christ, part of the gospel as well as bearer of it. The Church is not simply a convenient way of worshipping God together; nor is it a club for the like-minded. The glory of a local congregation is that it contains within it the unlike-minded, people of many and varied kinds: old and young, married and single, men and women, conservatives and socialists, working class and middle class, black and white, optimists and pessimists, and so on. What gives them their unity is their shared faith in Jesus Christ and their common

83

humanity. Here, in this sort of community, persons can grow and develop. In this way the Church is both sacramental – it is the bearer of the grace and presence of Christ – and also a sign of the Kingdom of God. The Church is never a perfect sign, and like all signs it is fragile: the community will have its moments of conflict and crisis as all human groups do. Learning how to resolve those crises without destroying the unity is what Christian discipleship is about. As the local church does this the values of the Kingdom – fraternity and community – are learnt, incarnated, and displayed.

What do Christians learn and practise?

First, the Christian community learns that each is dependent upon the other. In worship and fellowship each gives and receives. Members make different and unequal contributions – yet each gift is valued, even the lowliest: ' . . . the parts of the body which seem to be weaker are indispensable . . . ' (1 Cor. 12:22). The gifts are given for the 'common good' (12:7). There is no question of uniformity of vocation: each has his or her own distinctive calling (12:28). Yet equally the concept of the autonomous individual has no place in the eucharistic community.

Moreover, the health of the community as a whole is affected for good or ill by the health of the constituent parts. 'If one member suffers, all suffer together; if one member is honoured, all rejoice together' (12:26). Above all, the community learns to 'bear one another's burdens and so fulfil the law of Christ' (Galatians 6:2). It does not matter whether each member knows intimately or even very well all other members; but it does matter that each values the others as fellow members of the body and is concerned that each one should be able to play a full part, giving and receiving. In this way there is at the heart of every eucharistic community an underlying egalitarian predisposition. The Christian community rightly resists any attempt by particular people or groups to dominate or marginalize others – a lesson which the Corinthian congregation had to apply to the conduct of its communal and eucharistic meals (1 Cor. 11). It is this egalitarian predisposition which eventually compels Christians to confront slavery, racism, poverty and sexism.

In other words, there are most important insights to be gained here about the interdependence of communities, about how people who are very different, who make very different and unequal contributions, can nevertheless co-operate with one another in creating a *koinonia*, a fellow-ship, where everyone is enabled to play a part, no one is disabled, made invisible or excluded, and yet there is no question of uniformity or of each particular person being absorbed into the whole. In this way the Christian community envisages (or imagines) what the Kingdom of God is like, and the directions in which the wider society must go if those same values are to be realized there also.

What kind of a society do we want to see? One that recognizes human interdependence and enables all people to play a part, to make their different and unequal yet valued contributions; one where no one is disabled or made invisible or excluded and where there are limits to the permitted inequalities between people and groups; and one which promotes community by encouraging a sense of belonging to one another, a sense of obligation towards one another, a concern for the common good.[22]

This is not an impossible dream, because in parishes across the country Christians ought to be able to point to their own local congregations as living signs and parables of such a way of living. This is not to say that the wider society can be envisaged as simply a local congregation writ large; that would be absurd. But it is to suggest that if the Church is a sign of the Kingdom then there are clues in its corporate life about the way human beings must live together in the wider society if all people are to flourish – clues which lay Christians must take and develop in their secular vocations. This latter point about lay vocation is quite crucial and one which Catholicism – which is always tempted towards clericalism – too easily overlooks. The incarnational ministries of the last century and the earlier part of this, to which Catholics often refer, were largely clerical; the incarnational ministries of the present and future have to be largely lay.

What I envisage here, therefore, is that every local congregation should be encouraged to see itself as a centre of alternative living and imagining in a society which is

85

retreating from the ethic of fraternity and the insight of community. Each local church is a place of counter-culture – but not in the sense of providing a place of withdrawal. On the contrary, Catholics go out from their worship knowing that the sphere of redemption of the incarnate God is the whole world and the mission of the Church is likewise to the whole world.

Conclusion: the 'enabling state'

As we move towards the new century I think we are bidding farewell to the welfare state as we have known it and to more collectivist solutions to problems: people want to see less involvement by government at both local and national level. We need to envisage society in a new way. But we do not want to envisage a society which, in the name of freedom and the individual, is given over to an unregulated market economy – for such a society carries within it the seeds of its own destruction. We need a vision of what I would want to call an 'enabling state'. I accept the criticisms of the welfare state, its bureaucratic tendency, its creation of dependency – and of the free market, its inability to satisfy such basic needs as a house for everyone, its encouragement of atomistic, acquisitive individualism. An 'enabling state' is one which recognizes that both government (that is, collective action) and the market have parts to play in allocating social goods, though it is not doctrinaire about what those parts are and when it is most appropriate for either the market or collective action. It also recognizes that you cannot have markets without such associated properties as profits and incentives and that, as a result, there will have to be regulation and intervention to prevent gross inequalities. The test is whether the more market-orientated economy is serving the ends of fraternity and community, whether basic needs are being met, whether a sense of mutual obligation is being fostered and whether the constituent parts of society are able to participate in its life – for if they are not then the whole will ultimately be affected.

What sort of a society are we envisaging now? The social vision of our Catholic predecessors was right in regarding the economic order as made for people, and not people for the economic order. They were right in saying that it is by its effect on persons that a particular economic order should be judged. But times have changed, and our contribution towards renewing the nation's social vision must now acknowledge the failure, at least for the present, of many socialist economic and political projects. The social vision now goes beyond both a welfare state and a *laissez-faire* economy to that of an 'enabling state' where both markets and collective action have a part to play in helping persons to flourish. To this we contribute our understanding of what it is to be a person, our understanding of how persons are interdependent in the human community, and our understanding of how persons who are so different can nevertheless live together in unity.

1 See A.J. Elliot and Ian Swanson (eds), *The Renewal of Social Vision*, Occasional Paper no. 17, Centre for Theology and Public Issues (Edinburgh, 1989).

2 David Marquand, 'The Life after Death of Socialism', the *Guardian*, 5 June 1991. According to the former cabinet minister, Nicholas Ridley, the retreat from 'Thatcherism' has already begun. The fourth term would have seen further 'opting out' in education and health. 'This is very different from the current search for public services which are so good that no one will want to use the private sector' (Nicholas Ridley, *My Style of Government*, Hutchinson, 1991).

3 Ruth Kenyon, 'The Social Aspect of the Catholic Revival', in N.P. Williams and Charles Harris (eds), *Northern Catholicism: Studies in the Oxford Centenary and Parallel Movements* (SPCK, 1935), p. 375.

4 Charles Raven, *Christian Socialism 1848–1854* (1920), p. 21.

5 Kenyon, *op. cit.*, p. 379.

6 Ibid., p. 377.

7 Ibid., p. 379.

8 Ibid., p. 385.

9 E. Carpenter, *Church and People 1789–1889* (SPCK, 1937), p. 317.

10 See Francis Penhale, *Catholics in Crisis* (Mowbray, 1986).

11 Quoted in Gerhard Lohfink, *Jesus and Community* (SPCK, 1985), pp. 1–2. There were, of course, parallel movements to social Catholicism in both Protestant churches and the Roman Catholic Church. In the United States, liberal Protestants embraced the 'Social Gospel'.

12 Quoted in Adrian Hastings, *A History of English Christianity 1920–1985* (Collins, 1987), p. 174. For a résumé of the Christian Socialist movement in the nineteenth and twentieth centuries see R.H. Preston,

Church and Society in the Late Twentieth Century: the Economic and Political Task (SCM, 1983), pp. 13–32.

13 See D.G. Peck, *Catholic Design for Society* (Dacre Press, 1940), p. 11

14 A.M. Ramsey, *The Gospel and the Catholic Church* (Longmans, 1956), p. 180. See Kenneth Leech, *The Gospel, the Catholic Church and the World: the Social Theology of Michael Ramsey* (The Jubilee Group, 1990).

15 See George Carey, 'Parties in the Church of England,' *Theology* (July 1988), pp. 266–7.

16 Peck, op. cit., p. 13.

17 M.B. Reckitt (ed.), *Prospect for Christendom* (Faber, 1943), p. 251.

18 C.S. Lewis, *Christian Behaviour* (1943), p. 45, quoted in Kenneth Leech, *The Social God* (Sheldon Press, 1981), p. 26.

19 Leech, *The Social God*, p. 6.

20 *The Forgotten Trinity*, British Council of Churches, 1989.

21 Ibid., p. 22. See also the Board for Social Responsibility report, *Changing Britain: Social Diversity and Moral Unity* (1987), ch. 3, 'Persons in Community'.

22 See John Atherton, *Faith In The Nation: A Christian Vision for Britain* (SPCK, 1988).

5 Being Ourselves*

Jack Dominian

How does our faith help us towards – or hinder us from – being ourselves? Here I want to look at the current situation in this country, and in large parts of Western society in which people find themselves interested in God, but disenchanted with the churches. What kind of behaviour follows from such a tension? How is Christianity to respond to a situation in which its teaching, ranging from the ten commandments through the gospels, is overtly ignored and yet men and women want to behave in a moral way?

In particular, I want to explore an area which is rarely looked at, namely, to examine the findings of cognitive and dynamic psychology, which has given a wealth of information as to how our behaviour is shaped through our natural development, without any reference to God. This is precisely where we are. We are living in a society where nature dictates human behaviour. It is no longer controlled by Christian principles, and so we have to look at the older tradition of how grace influences nature, and in order to do this we need to understand better how uninfluenced nature operates.

As an introduction, let me state the psychological framework of references I shall use. There are two systems which I utilize. The first and more important is the dynamic point of view of Erik Erikson, John Bowlby, D.W. Winnicott, and others. The second is the contribution of cognitive psychologists, Piaget and Kohlberg. I shall start with some of the contributions of psychoanalytic theory,

*© Jack Dominian 1991

and will rely heavily on Erikson, but first I want to refer to the work of John Bowlby.

John Bowlby, who died recently, was a British psycho-analyst who paid much attention to the attachment tie between the mother and the child. Following ethological work, in which animals are seen to stay close and follow their mother, Bowlby postulated that there was a basic attachment between mother and infant. This is established in the first few weeks of life by means of biological par-ameters. The infant is attached to the mother through vision by recognizing her face and then the rest of her body, through sound by becoming familiar with her voice and recognizing it instantly, and through touch by holding and being held. In this way the baby becomes emotionally attached. This emotional attachment is fundamental for survival. It keeps the child close to the mother, and through crying, which evokes an instant response from the mother, its needs are met.

This basic attachment to the mother is a prototype of all attachments from birth to death. The relationships we form with friends and our future spouse are mediated by a profound bond we form with others. This is the foun-dation for the stability of marriage, and when Jesus pro-claimed the indissolubility of marriage he may well have been referring to this fundamental bond between two people. This strong unit of attachment is the foundation on which all our counselling to keep marriages intact is based. So when we appeal for marital stability in the name of Christianity we are making contact with a basic human tendency which is stronger than the vicissitudes of human feelings and conflict. There is a meeting point between Christian belief in indissolubility and the human tendency for attachment. Attachment by itself is not sufficient to preserve all bonds, otherwise there would be no divorce, but Christian teaching has a solid infrastructure to rely on.

We move on now to the first years of life. Picture the infant in the arms of its mother, being held, fed, played with, nurtured in the widest sense of the word. Erikson claims that in the depths of this experience the sense of trust is established. The roots of this trust are first physical. We feel unsafe when we are cold, hungry and tired. When we are picked up and held, we are given the sensation of safety. This safety is embodied in the person of mother and father, and gradually it expands. As we acquire language our trust increases to the verification of meaning, and gradually of deeds, so that we have to trust our parents physically, cognitively and linguistically.

Trust plays a major part in life. Without trust, there can be no human relationships, no co-operation in groups, no business enterprise; in fact, no human activity can take place. Against trust we have to set betrayal, and we all know how profoundly we feel let down when anyone does that to us, but particularly those close to us whom we trust. In the field of sexuality and marriage, in which I have taken a special interest, I want to draw to your attention that fidelity is a human inclination, not because Christianity forbids fornication and adultery, but because unfaithfulness and sex without love are betrayals of the integrity of trust. When Jesus rules against adultery he is basing his teaching on sound human foundations.

In fact, we would not have Christianity itself were it not for human trust. The apostles were receptive of Jesus' words and actions, and these provided such a sense of trust and wonder that they made an indelible impact. Without the sense of trust, there could not be Christianity. It is a human experience we can appeal to, and through it our sense of trust of God emerges. At the present moment human beings in the West are prepared to risk trusting God, but not the churches, and in this decade of evangelization we have to ask whether the God we project is the one who makes sense to our fellow human beings, and this should be a source of considerable concern to us.

Back to the developing child. We reach the second and third year of life. Many of you will have memories of your own children at this stage, or will be reliving these years through your grandchildren. This is the stage that Erikson calls autonomy. You can easily see why he uses this term. This is the time when the child achieves independence on a wide front of skills. It learns to use language, feed and dress itself, and play extensively. When these skills are acquired efficiently there is the satisfaction of effective accomplishment, but in the process of these developments children make many mistakes. The shoe is put on the wrong foot, the food all over the face and on the floor, and locomotion is learned with many falls. These mistakes may be accompanied by feelings of doubt and shame as we stumble and learn through trial and error. But learning new skills does not stop at the age of two or three. We are learning new things all our life, and coupled with this experience is self-esteem on the one hand and uncertainty, doubt and shame on the other.

From the psychological point of view, other things are happening during this phase which are important for our humanity and our faith. The young child leaves the side of the mother and goes to the next room where it plays happily alone. You may think that there is nothing unusual in this, but in fact it brings out a significant human experience. The child has learned to feel safe in the absence of the physical presence of mother. In technical terms it has internalized mother, or in ordinary language, preserves her presence in her physical absence. She lives inside the psyche without being present. This is a process which is invaluable for our humanity. We function as fully human because we remember those who matter to us in their physical absence. We leave home in the morning, and carry within us the reality of our family all day long. This is the way we retain our loved ones when they die.

Even more significantly, from the point of view of faith, the process of internalization, taking people in and holding on to them in their physical absence, is the way we acquire the sense of God. We do not see, touch or hear God. We are informed of his presence from the earliest stages of life, and slowly we internalize God within ourselves. The sense of God we actually internalize depends on the image of God that is given to us. This is where the Christian community has a crucial role to play. Do we impart a God of might and power, or a Father who loves and is benevolent? Whatever God we present, that is the one we assimilate. Internalization has nothing to do with reason and logic. It is a psychological process of taking inside us a person, and it shows us that Christianity has the means of transmitting the sense of God because the psychological process of registering this reality is available to everybody.

The third element of the second and third years, the phase of autonomy, is another interaction with mother and father. These are the years when the child is exploring the whole world around. It wants to touch everything within reach and do things which are forbidden. The sequence of events is that the child does something which is disapproved of and is told to desist. If it persists, there is a shout, and even a smack. At that moment the child experiences two emotions. It feels bad and guilty. Now badness and guilt might appear to be two words that are prerogatives of the Judaeo-Christian faith. Not so. They belong to humanity as a whole, and are experienced by the young child. The words basically apply to the rupture of the relationship between child and parent, and in terms of the Christian faith badness and sin are due to the rupture in the relationship between God and individual men and women.

Shortly after the rupture, the child feels cut off, and in human terms experiences rejection, is in fact temporarily out of paradise. All this is familiar language for the Christian faith. Within a short time, the child is forgiven, reconciliation takes place, and the relationship is restored to its pristine state. The child now feels good and the polarity between goodness and badness settles on humanity for everybody and for all time. Most of our life we either feel good or bad. In Christian terms, this has been related to sin, but the experience is absolutely basic to our humanity. Guilt too is related to the moment when we feel cut off from someone we love. This is vital to remember because for many Christians, particularly of the Roman Catholic tradition, guilt is associated with breaking rules, church rules. We need to remind ourselves that long before we learn to feel guilty about breaking rules we feel guilty when we have hurt someone we love, and at the heart of guilt is the rupture of personal relationships.

In the fourth and fifth years, the child goes through a phase of initiative. It explores the world around and learns to take the initiative. Even more important, as the first five years are negotiated the child becomes much more conscious of unconditional acceptance, that is to say, self-esteem is built on the feeling of being unconditionally accepted. Self-esteem is intimately linked with love of self. The child is being bombarded during these early years with good feelings. It feels lovable simply because it exists. This is the basis on which we graft God's unconditional love of us. We are conditioned to unconditional love, and the whole wonder of the cosmos of God's love for each one of us as an act of pure benevolence can be experienced by us because by the time we are four or five we have tasted unconditional love in our life. We know what it means to feel loved simply because we exist, without having to earn it. I need hardly remind you that the whole theology of arguments of earned and unearned grace which shook the Reformation is played out in these early years when we acquire the sense of unconditional love.

On reaching five we go to school where, according to Erikson, the child acquires the sense of industry. The school child learns the three Rs and begins the journey that will ultimately lead to work, but something more important is happening during the school years. We all learn at school a second way of acquiring our self-esteem, through our own efforts in a world where we are assessed continuously and given marks and ratings for our efforts. The achievements at school have important implications for our capitalist society. It is a society which rewards achievement, competition and results. Self-esteem is built on these efforts, with very little room for unconditional love. In fact, the ordinary man and woman who is busy with survival has very little time for the sense of unconditional love, and therefore the presence of God in their life. Life seems to be a struggle for survival, and the God that Christianity preaches adds very little to wages, the daily struggle for life, or paying the mortgage. Our society seems to divide self-esteem into that earned at work, which is the predominant experience, and that felt at home where unconditional love still prevails. That is why I advocate an evangelization thrust which depends on the home. The home is where the unconditional love of life is experienced through the spouse and can be brought within the orbit of God's unconditional love of us.

School is also the place where children are plunged into a world of community life. There they learn to adjust to community rules and the principles of law. In addition, up to the time of school the child is the person who receives love from parents. Through imitation it can attempt to give back love to its parents and can be loving to a young sibling, but it has not got the possibility of taking the initiative of loving. At school, and particularly towards the end of the primary school and the beginning of secondary school, it has the possibility of taking the initiative towards the children in a mutual way. Thus love of neighbour, which starts with parents, now enters the life of the child towards the second half of the first decade.

At about twelve or so puberty takes place, and the child, who is gradually separating from parents all the time, is now pubertal and the final phase of separation, which is sexual, occurs. Nature ensures that we separate from our parents and form our separate identity. After a period of separation we fall in love, and the process of attachment completes the cycle of human development from the dynamic point of view.

Before considering the process of moral development from the cognitive point of view of Piaget and Kohlberg, I would like to point out that the dynamic outline I have given you offers a framework within which God can operate. Humanists, of whom there are an increasing number, will say that we do not need a God for a moral system of life. The genetic contribution and environmental upbringing makes us fully human, without the need of God. Indeed, the protagonist of the psychoanalytic model, Freud himself, believed that God was a projection, the universal neurosis of mankind. There is an answer to that, but all I want to do at this point is to show that we have in our human model a framework on which God can be grafted, and from the religious point of view we need to say that if human beings are created in the image of God it should not be surprising that the language and concepts of religion should have a fertile soil in our humanity.

The cognitive model as we have it today is the work of

Piaget and Kohlberg. These two psychologists gave children stories and games and examined how they responded to the values involved. As a result of their studies they outlined a progressive evaluation of right and wrong. From an absolutist heteronomous obedience to authority to an independent autonomous decision-making; from a hedonistic selfish pleasure principle to a concern for others; from a concrete, materialistic, instrumental way of living life to one of mutual concern in which motivation plays a part.

As far as Piaget is concerned, I want to draw your attention to one feature that stands out. Up to the age of seven or eight children may say 'No' to suggestions from parents, may in fact rebel, but ultimately they will accept the dictates of parental authority. After the age of eight or thereabouts, they will want to question closely the demands that parents make on them and assess whether these demands are fair and just. The sense of mutuality arrives towards the end of the first decade, and children will not only challenge authority but they want to see it as just before they obey it.

This move from heteronomy to autonomy has had profound implications for the Roman Catholic Church. Indeed, it has implications for all the Christian churches. It would be true to say that the Roman Catholic Church behaved before the Second Vatican Council with a collective response to authority which placed it at a psychological level of up to the age of ten. There was an absolute obedience to authority which reflected the young child's response to parents. Since the Vatican Council the collective age of the Church has moved forward to the second decade of life. Now Roman Catholics want to evaluate the teaching of authority, and find it difficult to accept the arbitrary decisions of Rome. In fact, there is a real tension between Rome and the rest of the Church at this very level. There is a real danger on the other hand that if a church allows the autonomy of its members then there is utter confusion with no consensus. In practice what I would favour is that the Christian community reaches a consensus on religious truths and has a hierarchy which teaches with authority, having consulted its members. In that respect the churches with episcopal structures have an ability to hold themselves together, which is necessary at this particular time when all churches are at a low ebb.

Kohlberg defines moral development in terms of stages. Stage 1 is when fear predominates and obedience is based on it. In stage 2 decisions are made on the basis of pleasure. In stage 3 the influence of the group is paramount, and in stage 4 the law plays the ultimate part. What all these stages lack is autonomy in judgement. Basically the point is that if a person spends his life doing what he has been told to do by authority merely because of fear or for pleasure, or because it is expected by the group, or because that is the law, he has never really made a moral decision which is his own moral judgement.

This view has monumental implications for Christianity in our own time. Gone are the days when the community accepted the Judaeo-Christian tradition implicitly. Our responsibility as a Church is to encourage a mature moral decision, or in religious terms a decision of the mature conscience which is influenced by the Gospel. The task of the Church is now no longer to influence society to accept unconditionally the Christian message, but to have a dialogue in which the message is delivered in a persuasive manner and bears an influence on men and women as they make mature decisions about their lives.

It seems to me that Christianity, having been rejected as the received wisdom, is nurturing its bruised hurt and withdrawing into itself. The exception is the fundamentalist group of Christians who are proclaiming the Gospel loud and clear, but this is a voice doomed to failure because it is proclaiming a Gospel to an audience which is treated as being emotionally under the age of ten!

The way forward is to proclaim the Gospel in a way that is in dialogue with mature individuals who choose its proclamation as a mature, adult decision. The Gospel has to dialogue with the maturity of Western society, a dialogue between gospel truths and reasoned response. That is where society is today, and this is the way forward, both as a Church and in our individual handling of men and women who want to reach the truth.

6 Belonging to God*

Mother Allyne CSMV

> *Then Moses said to God, 'If I come to the people of Israel and say to them, "The God of your fathers has sent me to you," and they ask me, "What is his name?" what shall I say to them?' And God said to Moses, 'I AM who I AM'. (Exodus 3:13–14)*

> *Jesus said to them, 'Truly, truly, I say to you, before Abraham was, I am.' (John 8:58)*

Belonging is about relationship and identity. And belonging to God means (if we take as our understanding of belonging the definitions given us in the *Oxford Dictionary*) to accompany, to pertain to, to relate to, to be connected with, to form part of, to adhere to, the One who in the beginning said, 'Let there be'; the One who is, who calls forth Life; the One who calls forth *me*. It is to relate and adhere to the Source of all life; to desire One who is utterly other, yet who is revealed in that which we can see and hear and touch. Those who find their source in Life become in turn a source of life.

In our consumer society, 'belonging' tends to have strong associations with ownership, but there is nothing in today's possessive materialism which finds resonance in God. He is who he is, and will be who he will be; he is always in relationship, both within himself in the ceaseless sharing of love in the blessed and glorious Trinity, and with his creation. And we partake of God's nature, God's relating, through and in our belonging: our belonging to One who is the Way, whose very Being is in movement, drawing us into a deeper exploration of the mystery and wonder of all that is. This movement of belonging, of adhering and relating, is conveyed in Hebrew by the preposition 'to' or 'towards'. Our belonging is to be perceived and lived as an orientation, or movement or action *towards* God; a dynamic between creature and Creator in which the Creator also is 'towards' that which he creates – expressed wonderfully for me in Ezekiel 2:1: 'Son of Man, stand upon your feet and I will speak with you.' The One who creates me is ever speaking the creative word which I am; is ever creating, through the dynamic of love, a dynamic in which I am to stand on my feet and have a share.

Belonging is not static. Rather, it is something to be lived; something we both have and are on the way to. It lies at the heart of what we are about because it is at the heart of who we are – who we are towards God, towards each other, towards the Church, towards the world. Belonging such as this makes it possible to take risks, risks in our understanding, which propel us into new places. In Genesis 12:1–3 our belonging, our being towards God is placed firmly in the context of all the families of the earth.

> Now the Lord said to Abram, 'Go from your country and your kindred and your father's house to the land that I will show you. And I will make of you a great nation, and I will bless you, and make your name great so that you will be a blessing . . . by you all the families of the earth shall bless themselves.'

Our belonging and our identity are here fused into one. They have a purpose beyond themselves. One relationship compels us to recognize the existence of others. At the heart of our faith is no exclusiveness, no separation from that which was made through him 'without whom was not anything made that was made' (John 1:3). We belong to this world; we are towards it because it is of God, because God is towards it. And within that context, we belong to a particular family, a priesthood of believers, the Church:

> Now therefore if you will obey my voice and keep my covenant, you shall be my own possession among all peoples; for all the earth is mine, and you shall be to me a kingdom of priests and a holy nation. (Exodus 19:5,6)

Belonging to God calls us into being as a priestly people, mediating God to all the families of the earth. And so we are to be a sign of the relationship which exists between the Creator and all that he has made.

But God goes further. God ever goes further! Our being towards him is rooted in a particular place, a particular congregation, a particular community where the 'glory of the Lord is revealed' and all 'see it together' (Isaiah 40:5). 'You shall seek the place which the Lord your God will choose out of all your tribes to put his name and make his habitation there; thither you shall go.' (Deuteronomy 12:5)

Finally, there is the deep call to each one of us to be; to live in longing towards God, orientated towards God in all things, abiding in the One who is All-Holy, All-Mighty, and yet chooses to abide and to pitch his tent in me; to create and break and re-make his likeness in me. And as this paschal mystery is accomplished over and over again I become one who shares ever more deeply the knowledge that 'I am who I am'. My life, my being and that of the One towards whom I long become inseparable.

This creating, breaking and re-making is an intrinsic part of belonging to God, and it makes of the relationship something which is in turn wondrous, painful, baffling, uncomfortable, challenging, disturbing, awesome, and often really very funny. The more we adhere and are towards God, the more we allow ourselves to be addressed by the Truth, and in doing so allow God to be God in our life, to accomplish in us what we deem impossible – to surprise us!

By opening ourself to this lived mystery we come to understand what it is to be 'known', to be loved with the passionate tenderness and intimacy, the jealous yearning of the God who is towards us and who delights in us; a love which we both flee from and reach forward to embrace. God yields himself, empties himself, leads us with the bands of love; while we, faced with the enormity and all-consuming fire of such a love, live out our tendency to seek refuge not so much under the shadow of his wings as in committees and strategic planning! No doubt such things are necessary to our life and mission but they can so dominate our thinking, we can so hide behind them, that we starve in the midst of the lavish plenty which is held out to us – that is, a love which ravishes us, which brings us to a place of knowing, where we can say with Job: 'I have heard of thee by the hearing of the ear, but now mine eye sees thee' (Job 42:5). The inner eye beholds the fullness of its desire.

We are offered a share in the redeeming work of Christ in us and in the world around us, and through that a participation in the divine nature. We, the branches, share the total life of the vine, and that life is both a present possession and a future hope. The Holy One tabernacles in us while we are yet sinners, making of *us* the living Word of God in the world today. We are a pledge, a sign and an instrument of the Kingdom, and, as Word, as language, we are ever changing as society draws forth from us new responses, new expressions, rooted in the dynamic tradition we have inherited. A dynamic tradition which is ever bringing to birth.

Religious communities, too, are called into being as a sign, a sign to the Church of the true nature of the Church, just as the Church is called into being as a sign to the world of the true nature of the world. *Any* kind of lasting Christian commitment is in itself a sign to a world which doubts the existence of permanent values. Such a sign becomes a point of entry for Christ in the world, a sacrament. Above all, the sign we are called to be is that which shows forth the absolute claim of God on our lives, and our total orientation towards God, in whom we have and find our being. We are to be a living statement of God's sovereignty in creation, at odds with the idol of power possessiveness.

There is a story, I think from the Desert Fathers, which sums up the experience of being a religious. An interested observer approached a monk one day and said, 'Tell me, what do you actually *do* in the monastery?' And the monk

101

thought for a moment and then said, 'We fall and we rise; we fall and we rise; we fall and we rise.'

That very descriptive answer, which all of us, I think, would recognize as a pattern in our own life, removes very effectively the romantic, other-worldly glow that often is placed on the religious life. Basically, a religious community, like the Church to which it belongs, is a fellowship of sinners, striving to live in truth before God and before each other, following along the Way, living out the baptismal commitment it shares with the people of God, yet in a particular and distinctive manner. We fall short, we fail, we make mistakes, and we learn to forgive over and over again; for true community is founded on and sustained by forgiveness, by love and reverence for one another and for the things of God. Personally and corporately, we are in a state of incompleteness moving towards completion, towards God, along a Way which involves risk, which involves change and growth. This process is an unavoidable part of belonging to God.

Rapid change has been a dominant feature of our world over the last few decades, and the Church too has known much change, though hardly so rapid! Religious communities also, despite the fact that those who have little or no contact with us tend wrongly to believe that we are the bastions of a tradition which is an iron-collar perpetuation of the past, have been living through profound and often radical change since the 1960s. And living, as we do, with the personal and corporate effects of the process of change (and it must be said that the process is very often more painful than the change itself) twenty-four hours a day, seven days a week, 'for the rest of our life in this world' (as the rite of Profession puts it), we know what it is to live with tension. We know too, and can boldly proclaim to a Church which has much present tension and uncertainty, that such a state *can* be healthy and creative. It is not necessarily unhelpful. Yes, our unity may be constantly vulnerable to attack, but we are assured that the powers of death shall not prevail against it. Change, or rather the threat and fear of change, can, and in my experience does, produce discontinuity, disruption, isolation and a feeling of alienation. Above all it can culminate in a polarizing of views and the consequent inevitable distortion and loss of truth. But from this place of breaking, of seeming destruction, we learn to live with the ambiguities and paradoxes at the heart of the gospel, with the richness and diversity of the community (or of the Church). It is a movement towards maturity, towards the 'measure of the stature of the fullness of Christ.'

Religious communities have been experiencing in part a systematic breaking down of long-established assumptions and of the outer fabric of their life – not least in the dismantling of institutional works. It has been uncomfortable and bewildering; at times it has felt life-threatening. It has left us with many questions and few answers, with a deep longing for, and awareness of our need of, God. Holding in balance, in creative tension, the participation of Christ's self-emptying, his self-surrender, and the fullness of life which is promised in him, is not and has not been easy. It brings personal and corporate conflict, and challenges us to live at the point of the cross where opposites are united but not dissolved. It ensures that that one-sidedness which alienates us from ourself and from what we are called to become, does not prevail. In the midst of profound change and transition we are brought to a place of paradox where the feeling of accelerated change brings also a sense of impasse. We yearn for a clearly defined path of life; to know who and what we are, to discern where we are going. This place of impasse is a place of discernment, prayer and hope, as we wait, our luggage discarded, ready to move. The future awaits our response. In the meantime, we are still standing, we are still walking together along the Way with hope and great joy.

Confusion, chaos, challenge, are so often the outcome of an encounter with Christ in the gospel. Yet even so Christians tend, on the whole, still to perceive calm waters as the presence of God and profound discomfort as the absence of Christ's peace. It may be that this is sometimes the case, but it is also, I believe, more often a reflection of our tendency to try to contain God, to make of him our own possession – to try to tame the One who is a consuming fire, who will always burst forth from our imprisoning images.

Being towards God involves us in a relationship with One who is a profound disturber of our person and of the *status quo*. We are constantly challenged to perceive and understand continuity in our lives through seeming discontinuity and disruption. Over and over again we are confronted with the truth of who we are and are called on further – 'I go before you into Galilee.' And the truth of who we are has both present reality and future hope. Our grasp of it is always partial. So even the truth we have is constantly being shattered and challenged lest we make of what is partial something that is absolute. The mighty are brought down, and along with them the comfortable systems which were built on truth but which, once embodied, once static, become hollow.

Religious communities have had to learn to stay with darkness, emptiness and uncertainty in relation to both their present and future. It has been a necessary part of God's making and remaking of us. Certainly it would have been more comfortable to have reached out for easy solutions – that is, short-term solutions. Had we done so (and the danger of doing so still remains) we would have missed the opportunities which have been offered, the life which is even now bursting forth. For behold, God *is* doing a new thing whether we perceive it or not. Our resources have been and still are overstretched, a situation which the Church also experiences; and we are often encumbered with buildings which both drain us and govern the way we live. But new ways of being towards God and the world are opening to us. There is a strong call, an urgent command, to live more provisionally, to let the future shape itself out of the passion of our present response, to let it come to us as the spring rains that water the earth!

This is the call and the challenge. We are to divest ourselves of so much that hinders us from running the race that is set before us. And when we have done so, I do not doubt that still another will strip us and gird us and lead us in a way we would not go. Our structures are not to be confused with the life itself. This we have learnt.

Our life and witness do not need justifying: God is to be our only justification. This we are learning. Above all, God does not need protecting! Rather we are to wrestle as Jacob wrestled with the Angel of God; to stand up on our feet and to speak face to face with the All-Holy; and perhaps even to be so bold as to remind him of his faithfulness.

We live in a time of social crisis, of change and of transition. If the Church also finds itself in crisis and change then perhaps we have cause to be thankful! At least it is still responding to the context in which God calls it into being. For belonging to this world which is God's is an intrinsic part of being towards God, and the Church and religious communities within it reflect intensively what is happening in their surrounding social and cultural context. They also, as living organisms, are constantly adapting to it, continually 'becoming' in relation to it. This process involves and requires a repeated turning to Christ – what Thomas Merton refers to as a 'total inner transformation', whereby we are seen to be passionate lovers of our Maker, partaking of God's glory, God's very Being, in the wounded, broken and disfigured of our world, whether poor, rich or middle class.

At one and the same time we are called to be in the wilderness where Christ is encountered in word, silence and sabbath, and at the edges where the coming of the Kingdom pushes out the boundaries of today's world. What the South American theologian Jon Sobrino says of religious communities rings true, and has perhaps some truth also for the Church: 'If religious life by its very structure involves a certain abnormality, then that life will experience crisis when it seeks to become normal and when it is no longer in the desert and on the frontier.'

The natural place for the people of God is in the desert and on the frontiers, the edges of our society, where our witness will proclaim the inclusive nature of the One to whom we belong. We have always to be wary of developing a ghetto mentality, whether from misunderstanding our purpose through an inadequate rooting of theology in life, or from fear and uncertainty, from protection of a past relationship or identity. The Spirit urges us to look beyond ourselves, to push not only the external frontiers in society, but the inner frontiers in our understanding: to live with the discomfort and challenge of other perceptions. Our sedentary, static faith is to be knocked silly into the light of the resurrection where we are compelled to believe beyond the evidence of our senses. Suddenly we discover 'he is not here', that 'he has gone before us', and we are propelled into movement, into 'forsaking what lies behind and reaching out for that which lies ahead'. Movement becomes an imperative, not an option.

This movement, this imperative, is a movement towards God, a part of what it means to belong. As we are urged out of the ghetto into which we have withdrawn, so our idols, our images of God are broken down. So deep-rooted are those images that we experience their loss as the loss of God rather than the place of beginning, the place of waiting in contemplative hesitation for the God who reveals himself. It is in this state of awaiting, of prayerful expectation, that we learn 'to let the "Come, Lord" of the Apocalypse rise up in our hearts day by day and to say "Come for mankind, come for me"' (R. Schutz). Whatever happens, we know we cannot return to where we were. We cannot return to the safety of the old days. In any case, if they have crumbled so easily, they were, after all, none too safe!

Speaking of the Church, Johannes Metz in *Followers of Christ* says:

> In the fear of an internal loss of meaning and of a growing lack of significance, our church life is placed between the danger of shutting itself off in a special religious world out of a spirit of faint-heartedness or even élitism, and the danger of over-adaptation to a world on whose definition and formation it hardly exerts any more influence.[1]

Pondering this statement I was reminded of something I read about twenty years ago, written, I think, by Sebastian Moore in *No Exit*: 'Poor old Church that has to learn from the world how to proclaim Christ to the world.'

Yes . . . and yet . . . in this world in which without him is not anything made that is made, God's Word is ever spoken in creation for those who have ears to hear. And for those who have eyes to see he reveals himself in that which he makes. Is his creation not crying out to us? Are his people not also? Do we not need to come forth from our secure places and to hear his voice calling us? Are *we* not in need of being evangelized by the Word which is being spoken in our world, in our society, in order that the universe, all in heaven and on earth, might be brought into a unity with Christ?

The world needs a people alive to God and therefore to each other – unafraid to say 'I feel', 'I love', 'I know', even 'I don't know' – a people which is human, of the earth as Christ was. Jesus can and does still quicken hearts to life, but does his body the Church do so? Do religious communities? Are we patterned on Christ? If we are, then we are summoned to love, to poverty of spirit, to single-ness of heart, to obedience, for these are not the domain of the religious life alone, but gospel imperatives to all who belong to God, who follow Christ by walking in his Way.

We are called to poverty of spirit, to giving unstintingly of ourselves, to being vulnerable to situations and people. And such a way of loving has practical implications. It requires the will not to possess; to witness in an age of materialism and greed to the need to recover a reverence for things and people; to live towards God in relation to all that he has made. We are called too to singleness of eye and heart, to purity and unpossessiveness in our relationships; to what Metz calls 'the expression of an uncompromising concentration of longing for the day of the Lord'. It has to do with being 'radically seized by and unreservedly engaged on behalf of the dominion of God that is at hand'. Like poverty of spirit, it has to do too with reverence for all that God has made, including our-selves, and it finds its outward expression in a heart which pours itself out: a heart whose eye is single.

> If I could wish for something
> I would wish for neither wealth nor power
> but the passion of possibility:
> I would wish only for an eye
> which, eternally young,

107

eternally burns
with the longing to see possibility!

S. Kierkegaard, 'The Moment'

Baptized into Christ, there is no other way for us than that of mature obedience, the decisive attitude in following Christ; our Yes, our assent to being one with him in his Yes – spoken with joy! In living out that assent, that yielding of all that we have and are towards God, our true nature is restored, and we are given the courage to say 'I am who I am', 'I will be who I will be'; and in doing so partake of God's very Being. In this we know ourselves to be sojourners and more than sojourners – pilgrims moving towards God, towards an end accomplished, a fulfilment and completion of our being. 'Be ye holy' – whole, complete – 'as your Heavenly Father is holy.'

It is easy enough to speak of assent, it is more complex in practice. We join and belong to things, adhere to certain precepts and groups, for a mixture of reasons. Even our *best* endeavours suffer weakness of purpose and confusion of motive, and the ground of our choice appears often to be confusion. But the more we face honestly the confusion in our choices (which is to face ourselves honestly, to have 'truth in the inward parts'), then the more those choices are gradually made from a place of greater understanding and freedom. Perhaps we can never expect to know ourselves fully; perhaps we will continue to see through a glass darkly, but being towards God involves us in a journey of painful, healing truth to a place of humility, of honest recognition.

This movement towards God expressed as a search and journey towards unity of being has traditionally been associated with the religious life. The word 'monk' itself comes from the word *monos* meaning 'one': one whose heart is undivided, whose eye is single. For those who live together in some form of monastic community, this single eye or undivided heart is not something for oneself alone, but is the possession of the whole body, the whole worshipping community. 'Those who live in unity in such a way that they form but one person are rightly called *monos*, one single person,' said Augustine.

We are 'of one heart and mind on the way to God'. Our sharing of all that we have and are, that is, our principle of community of goods (goods both material and spiritual), is not just an expression of life in community, but is to be a way of fellowship, a way of loving as well as a way of liberation, detachment, from possessiveness. To have one heart and one mind is a sign of hope in a divided society, but it is not an easily won unity. Nor is it a denial, a stifling of our diversity, a diversity which is part of the abundance and richness of God's gifting of us. Rather it comes about by our willingness both personally and corporately to live with and through the contradictions which lie deep within us. We are called to stand at the place of intersection, to stand like Moses 'in the gap', confident that every moment, every situation, whatever the circumstances, is a point of departure, an opening up and a path for the wind of the Spirit.

To stand in the gap (Ezekiel 22:30) is both part of what it means to live towards God and a sharing in the redeeming work of Christ at the points of intersection, of crisis, of contradiction. It is no easy place to stand. It is often profoundly disturbing. Almost everything in us would prefer to opt out of such discomfort by choosing one point of contradiction at the expense of the other; the result being an inevitable loss of truth. Holding the opposites in tension demands a willingness to wait on God like watchmen for the morning, prepared not to force conclusions before the *kairos*, the time that is God's time, when the 'truth between' will come to meet us. God the Holy Spirit is a disturbing reality, brooding over the waters of chaos, over the deep inner contradictions and ambiguities, in order to call forth life in its fullness. He is at work in the gap; the place of breakdown, of affliction, from which light and life burst forth.

The Hebrew word *pharatz*, meaning 'to break asunder', is full-deep with implication and holds this seeming contradiction together powerfully. It declares it One. The noun 'gap', which is rooted in this verb 'to break asunder', conveys a richness of meaning which certainly underlines and confirms my own lived experience: to tear down, demolish, to break asunder, to afflict (Job 16:14); but also to break forth as a child in the womb (Genesis 38:29); for water to burst forth (Job 28:4, Authorized Version) like a torrent; to spread abroad, increase, overflow. Yet at the same time this gap, this place of profound discomfort where we are asked to stand, is also a creek, a haven (Judges 5:17). Being towards God, belonging to Christ, will always bring us into the experience of the paschal mystery where we learn in Jesus that the grave is only a resting place, the void, the gateway to life. And in our willed content to stand in the place of affliction and of increase we come to new life.

However much we may acknowledge this, it is difficult not to be bogged down by the contradictions that are an inevitable part of the spiritual journey, and it sometimes seems that the emphasis we place on constant growth and on a linear evolutionary progress contributes paradoxically to the feeling of being stuck. Such an emphasis on portraying life in terms of linear growth may be well founded individually, socially and economically, but it can also produce a kind of holy fatalism; it can dull us to the urgency of our situation, to the crisis in which we await God's coming, to the crossing points where Christ dies that we might live, where we too must die if we are to live. For the world which God created and creates, to which we belong and in which we have a share, is formed by an evolutionary process which has at its heart the principle of interruption. It is the moment of interruption and the falling or breaking away of what no longer fulfils its purpose towards life, which provides the possibility of growth, of coming into being in response to external situations. This principle of interruption, of breaking down and bursting forth, is for me part of the experience of belonging to God. There is no way I can avoid the challenge of interruption, of change and transformation, of death and resurrection.

Sometimes in recent years, it has seemed that the process of interruption and change has been such that the very fabric of the religious life is being undermined. Responses to it have understandably ranged from pain, bewilderment and frustration to excitement, challenge and hope. How often have we heard the refrain, 'This is no longer the community I joined.' No doubt a refrain familiar to all in the Church! We must understand and respect the sense of loss which underlies such a statement, but it is surely right that it is 'not the same community'. There is a place for conservatism. But we must be conservative only in as much as we persevere in the radical following of Christ to which we are called. And that radical discipleship must be the touchstone by which we assess our life and traditions. Nothing living is static, and that which initially brings freedom, once enshrined, enslaves. To belong to Christ is in some sense to be committed to change in ourselves, change in others, change in the pattern and fabric of our life together, and it demands that we leave room for such change. Wherever we are, whatever the position we adopt, the person of Jesus Christ challenges the place we are in radically, to its very roots. Belonging to God, we are yet always on the way to God.

The religious life is a search undertaken freely and willingly; it comes into being through God's initiative, is sustained by God's continuing presence and is lived in faith. It is a continuous risking of oneself to an unknown future. Like the Church, religious communities try to live out a response to the gospel which is uncompromising while surrounded by a milieu of compromise. (As an aside, it is interesting to note that historically they seem often to have come into being not at times of great confidence in the Church but at times of uncertainty, even of disorientation.) At its best, the religious community is a charismatic sign in the Church of the radical following of Christ to which we are *all* called, and of the intrinsically human gift of being utterly absorbed in the religious dimension of life. That is, of perceiving all of life as under the reign of God.

A Directory of the Religious Life (1990), a document put forward by the Advisory Council on the Relations of Bishops and Religious Communities for the use of those concerned with the administration of the religious life in the Church of England, states the following common purposes for religious communities:

(a) to bear witness before and on behalf of the whole

111

human family, to God within and beyond all things and to the coming of his kingdom;

(b) to be signs, for those who have eyes to see, of the total commitment which Christ demands from all who would follow him;

(c) to express the God-given value of all right human relationships by offering the Christian commitment of love through their life in community;

(d) to be communities of worship where prayer to God is practised, and to be sources from which others may draw encouragement and inspiration;

(e) to give individual men and women freedom to devote themselves permanently to loving service of God in a disciplined common life;

(f) to stand alongside the poor, the exploited, the power-less and the marginalized, not only in ministry, but also in prayer, and to enter into their sufferings to whatever degree is possible.

By and large, the Anglican Church is not very aware of the religious life as an intrinsic part of the Church's life, and this very fact, while admittedly being often frustrating and discouraging, can give to religious communities a freedom to cross boundaries unhindered – boundaries between the institution of the Church and society, between denominations, between the variously labelled parties within the Anglican fellowship. Being on the fringe of the ecclesiastical establishment brings its own benefits!

Religious communities are being called on more and more to cross these boundaries both by the Church and by those who stand outside its orbit, thirsting yet doubtful of the establishment's ability to slake that thirst. There are increasing demands made on us for spiritual direction, teaching on prayer, preaching, retreat conducting, and these calls on us are much more than we can encompass. The Spirit is powerfully at work, stirring people to life. But this very movement, like all things, holds within it the possibility of distortion. There is the danger of increasingly seeing and portraying belonging to God as something private and personal rather than social. Can Christianity be that? It is first and foremost a revelation of relationship, of a call to be a *people*. All communities, whether parish congregations or religious communities, witness to this; and the witness of being a 'people' is greatly needed in our day.

Those who come to us seeking God, or seeking support and encouragement in their journey, or a deepening of their experience of God, come from the whole spectrum of the wider Church – Anglican, Roman Catholic, Protestant – and also from a place of non-alignment – the 'unchurched'. Increasingly from within the Anglican Church we are being turned to from what is commonly referred to as the Evangelical wing. Vocations too are coming less frequently from the Anglo-Catholic tradition, but more frequently from Evangelical and Free Church backgrounds. Something new and unusual is happening.

The Spirit is waiting to be released – to transform and surprise. This can be seen not only in the growing large numbers seeking times of quiet and reflection in monasteries and convents all over the country, but in the hidden, dedicated commitment and desire of an ever-increasing number of men and women testing their vocation as Oblates and Tertiaries, seeking a place of belonging, a context for the deep yearning that is within.

The hunger for God, the growing awareness of the need to see the whole of life and creation as sacrament, is very strong in our day and we need to take hold of it, to learn from it. We are constantly hearing and reading that we live in a post-Christian society. But I believe it to be a religious generation all the same. It asks the big religious questions; questions whose answers are only discovered in living through the questions. In reflecting on life and its meaning, it engages in theology – How, Why, What, Who? For the most part, it is a generation which has not been given the tools to handle such reflection. We have been happy to let theological reflection become almost solely the preserve of colleges and universities. Academic theology is needed and must be encouraged, but the basic tools are sadly needed in the streets and in the pews! People need to hear and understand that where they are is where God is; that the reality of the present is where the Word of God is at work searching to bring to light the things now hidden in darkness. If the Decade of

113

Evangelism achieves no more than to cast out the widely held view that until we have achieved some required level of goodness and holiness we cannot come before God, it will have done much. The message of free, unmerited mercy and love needs to be taken out from its hiding place and put on a lampstand for all to see.

Our society thirsts for the things of the Spirit. Such a thirst will not be assuaged by programmes of action, nor by a glimpse of a Church unnerved by media pressure, shaken by internal politics and seemingly absorbed by issues which at times appear irrelevant. While we spend so much of our energy in this way and proclaim increasingly our separate mentality, we deny the all-embracing length, breadth, height and depth of God. Belonging to God is undoubtedly to 'be longing towards God'. It is 'a venture of faith akin to a venture of love' (Hans Küng) in which we are ever seeking 'a deeper immersion in existence' (Kierkegaard). In worship, prayer and adoration we bow before the mystery at the heart of our world, of each other and of ourself. From this place of profound adoration and silence we recover the reverence for all things which can save our world and our society.

Abbot Lot came to Abbot Joseph and said, 'Father, according as I am able, I keep my little rule, and my little fast, my prayers, meditation and contemplative silence; and according as I am able I strive to cleanse my heart of thoughts: now what more should I do?' The elder rose up in reply and stretched out his hands to heaven, and his fingers became like ten lamps of fire. He said: 'Why not be totally changed into fire?'[2]

1 Johannes Metz, *Followers of Christ* (Burns and Oates, 1978).
2 Thomas Merton, *The Wisdom of the Desert* (Sheldon Press, 1973).

7 'Behold: I Make All Things New'*

Richard Holloway

I love the poems of A.E. Housman. He was a Cambridge don, a classicist – a rather pedantic one, it is said – and, like many of the old pagan poets he loved, he was a nostalgic pessimist. His poems ache with a sense of loss. Of his own poetry he wrote:

> They say my verse is sad: no wonder;
> Its narrow measure spans
> Tears of eternity, and sorrow,
> Not mine, but man's.[1]

But even more powerful than the nostalgia is the pessimism. It pervades his poetry, but occasionally a line leaps out like the slash of a sword, with unarguable decisiveness. Before I became familiar with Housman's poetry, I came across one of his sword thrusts quoted in G.K. Chesterton's autobiography and it has stuck in my mind ever since:

> The troubles of our proud and angry dust
> Are from eternity and shall not fail.[2]

One of the most enduring human illusions is that our current difficulties are abnormal, ought to pass soon and will be succeeded by an uninterrupted era of tranquillity. We expect life to be like the shuttle between Heathrow and Edinburgh, a smooth ride on the whole, interrupted by occasional bouts of turbulence, through which we are

*© Richard Holloway 1991

advised to fasten our seat belts. In fact, the human reality is the reverse of that. Turbulence is the norm, interrupted by occasional periods of tranquillity.

One reason why people endlessly predict the disintegration of the Anglican Church is because of the prevalence of this tranquillist heresy. The doctrine is that we have departed or fallen from a normative tranquillity and that our present troubles are abnormally stimulated by human wickedness and error, whereas it is the other way round. Turbulence and disagreement are the norm, the signs of life, and we should accept them as such. 'The troubles of our proud and angry dust are from eternity and shall not fail,' said Housman. But Job said it too: 'Man is born unto trouble, as the sparks fly upward' (Job 5:7).

Let us spend some time meditating on this claim. Let us look at some of the troubles of our proud and angry dust. A keen classifier of the troubles that afflict humanity might put them into at least five categories.

The first category that suggests itself is the *objective or external trouble*, like being caught in a violent storm. It is no accident that the endless struggles in Ireland have been known colloquially as 'the troubles' for longer than seems possible. Our forebears were clearer in their contemplation of the troubles that afflict vulnerable human beings, and their robustness was reflected in the Litany as they besought the Lord to deliver them from plague, pestilence and famine; from battle, murder and sudden death. Even in the comparatively user-friendly environment of the affluent West, human existence is troubled by factors beyond our control. I can still remember the pain and bafflement I felt when my mother was taken away to hospital when I was a boy, because of a mysterious woman's trouble that seemed to reach into our home and capture her from us. The precariousness and transience of human life is one of the great themes of the pagan poets loved by Housman, but it's there in scripture and it is the great subtext in St Augustine. In Peter Brown's marvellous biography of Augustine he writes:

All the sadness of the ancient philosophers will flood into Augustine's language as he talks of this transience. Human existence is 'a speck of rain compared with eternity'.

'Let a few years go by; let the great river slip forward, as it always does, passing through many places, washing, always, through some new tombs of the dead.'[3]

Nowadays we have devices for avoiding the knowledge of our own transience and trouble, and the new liturgies are more coy in expressing it, whereas the old books were plangently straightforward: 'Man that is born of a woman hath but a short time to live, and is full of misery. He cometh up, and is cut down, like a flower; he fleeth as it were a shadow, and never continueth in one stay.'

But these external troubles that define and end our human condition are not the only struggles we know.

A second category is our *internal subjective troubles*. We carry about within our own minds and souls whole landscapes and histories of pain and anxiety. Most of us spend a lot of time inside our own head in an unuttered commentary on the world and our own existence within it. Occasionally a brilliant novel or a good biography will tear off the mask from someone and reveal the inner narrative, but most of us are expert at not blowing our cover. Like spies deep in enemy territory, we live our double lives, camouflaging our anxieties, painting a shell over our shyness and self-doubt, moving warily through life like the commander of a Centurion tank in hostile territory.

The mysterious thing about these troubles is that they are part of the inner fabric of our nature. This is particularly true of the psycho-sexual problems that afflict us as human beings. Though not utterly determined by it, most of us are profoundly modified and sometimes radically wounded by our early conditioning and experiences. Philip Larkin was in no doubt about it:

> They fuck you up, your mum and dad.
>   They may not mean to, but they do.
> They fill you with the faults they had
>   And add some extra, just for you.

117

But they were fucked up in their turn
By fools in old-style hats and coats,
Who half the time were soppy-stern
And half at one another's throats.

Man hands on misery to man.
It deepens like a coastal shelf.
Get out as early as you can,
And don't have any kids yourself.[4]

I am increasingly impressed by the discoveries that modern psychology is making about the influence of early experience upon our subsequent lives. Most of us will escape the serious psychoses that afflict human nature, but few of us miss out on painful neuroses or personality defects that complicate our adult lives, ambushing us constantly, trapping us in inappropriate relationships, complicating our encounters with others, building mysterious rigidities and terrors into our nature.

Members of the Diocese of Edinburgh will know to their great boredom how impressed I have been recently by a book called *The Psychology of Military Incompetence*.[5] It is essentially a study of the authoritarian personality. The author, Norman Nixon, shows that behind many of the avoidable military disasters in history were officers who were crippled by authoritarianism. The author ascribes most of the problem to bad potty training. However we account for it, he is surely right in defining an authoritarian as possessing four distinct but related characteristics. The first of these is what the army calls 'bullshit', an obsession about spit and polish or ritualistic minutiae, captured by the sergeant-major who tells his recruits, 'If it moves salute it, if it don't move blanco it.' Or by his equivalent in the Anglo-Catholic underworld, the all purpose master of ceremonies, who coolly informs new priests, panic-stricken at celebrating their first High Mass, 'When in doubt say, "The Lord be with you".'

The second characteristic of the authoritarian personality is an excessive reverence for authority and precedence. This reverence is rooted in a profound anxiety about uncertainty and chaos. It creates the kind of mind for which a thing can never happen for the first time, encapsulated in the defensive anxiety of the woman who pronounced that she would never let her little Jimmy enter the water until he had learned to swim. Over the shoulder of the authoritarian's obsessive reverence for authority looms the disapproving parent, quick to find fault, terrible in wrath, so why risk it?

This is why the third characteristic, especially dangerous in a battlefield commander, is that fear of failure becomes a more controlling emotion than hope of success. The paradox of many military disasters is that they are bred more of caution than of risk-taking, more from fear of failure than the daring grasp at success. All the great military leaders, like all the great spiritual or intellectual leaders, are creative risk-takers whose aim in life is to achieve success rather than avoid failure; to find out what lies ahead, rather than put a ring fence round what they already know.

The fourth and perhaps the most tragic characteristic of the authoritarian personality is the inability to love or express profound emotion. We know that the ability to love is an original endowment from our parents. We love because we are first loved. The disapproving and unloving parent and the disapproving and unloving God produce the frigid, frightened personality, defined by coolness rather than warmth, negation rather than affirmation, disapproval rather than acceptance. We know that authoritarian personalities often find themselves in positions of leadership, in the Church as well as in the army. Indeed, there's probably a doctoral thesis to be written on the psychology of ecclesiastical incompetence, a case study in the authoritarian personality and the Anglo-Catholic movement. It is easier, of course, to recognize these symptoms in others than in oneself; to perceive the speck in our brother's eye, rather than the beam that is in our own. The point, anyway, is that the mature life is the examined life, the life that knows itself, its wounds as well as its strength.

If we are troubled by the psychological loading we receive from parents and society, we are even more disturbed by a third category of troubles: those which are bound up with the mysterious springs of *sexual identity* and its life-long reverberations. There is always, anyway, a tension between received values and the actuality of our own natures. We know from our own experience as well as our study of human nature that the most vociferous defender of a moral standard is often engaged in a painful inner struggle with it. This is particularly true of sexual standards, where human beings are prone to persecute in others what they most fear in themselves. The pain is acute enough for those who are afforded legitimate, if limited outlets for their passions, but what about those who are afforded none? Created sick, commanded to be sound; created gay, commanded to be straight. Sexual issues seem to be peculiarly intractable for the Christian community, with the gay dilemma exactly mirroring the dilemma over women's ordination. Each of them an allegedly impossible possibility, a created fact that cannot be hallowed, a reality that dare not speak its name. And this denial of undeniable reality cuts a great wound in us that cannot be healed, until we acknowledge the impossibility of the contradiction. I do not want to begin here a substantive discussion of these issues; I raise them only to illustrate the claim that the human condition is troubled from without and from within, by pains it does not seek and by pains it generates from within its own confusion.

A fourth category, and another most fruitful source of trouble for human beings, is *cognitive stress*, the anxiety produced by new knowledge and new human realities. We know how cognitive systems change in all disciplines. During periods of transition in knowledge systems there is intense pressure upon practitioners of particular disciplines, some of whom are scrupulously anxious to respond to new knowledge and feel intellectually displaced a lot of the time. Others enter recurrent phases of defensive stress, because they believed profoundly in the defeated systems and new knowledge is endlessly resisted. Since no one ever blows a whistle and calls a break in the evolution of knowledge, people in the field get very battered indeed.

One of the most contentious examples of contemporary cognitive stress is provided by the new reproductive techniques that permit children to be conceived by donor insemination from an anonymous father, whose perpetual anonymity is protected by current legislation. Even more radical are the techniques for embryo implantation, whereby the resulting child will have two legal parents and two genetic parents. A recent complicating element was distractingly added by the so-called 'virgin birth' case. But if we move from these unexplored rivers to more familiar waterways we encounter equally passionate resistance and turbulence, no matter how well we think we know about the issues.

Liturgical reform and the rearranging of our churches consequent upon it have been potent sources of trouble in many parishes; and eminent persons, not excluding the heir to the throne, take every opportunity to pour scorn upon the new and heap praise upon the old services. Indeed, one of the many ironies that have attended the business of liturgical reform is provided by the nostalgic ex-believer who likes to visit the old neighbourhood of faith once a year as a Christmas tourist and bitterly resents the changes that are found there. We find the same reaction when we seek to reappraise the function of redundant churches in the light of our total mission. The problem lies in the fact that the Christian Church down the centuries has become the incidental transmitter of much beauty in language, ornament and architecture. These are secondary aspects of the Church's primary purpose, but for many believers and ex-believers they have become its primary purpose. The preservation and transmission of beauty are important and may even be thought of as part of the Church's mission, but they are not the essential task of the Church so there are inevitable conflicts between the mission of the Church and the heritage movement.

We have all been involved in these struggles, which have to do with the externals of faith, but what about the theological troubles that have always characterized the

Christian community? Theological conflict seems to have been intrinsic to the Christian movement from the very beginning. Indeed, in the First Letter to the Corinthians Paul suggested that there had to be factions among us in order that the genuine may be recognized. Conflict is inescapable among lovers of and searchers for the truth, and matters of truth are never finally settled.

As I reflect upon my own theological history, without going into any depth, I can detect ten major theological movements that have influenced me in the last forty years. The first was the Neo-Orthodox movement associated with Karl Barth. Bracketed somewhere to the left of this were the Niebuhr brothers, Reinhold and Richard, who taught me much. Next there came, in contra-distinction to Barthianism, the demythologizing programme of Rudolf Bultmann, introduced to the English-speaking world by our own John Macquarrie, who went on to base a whole systematic theology upon the philospher who lay behind Bultmann's approach, Martin Heidegger. Then came the secular theologies of the 1960s – thin stuff this, but intoxicating, like cheap whisky. A more profound theology grew out of the Death of God movement with its winning slogan, 'There is no God and Jesus is his Son'. Don Cupitt is the heir to that movement and its most convincing exponent. For Cupitt, God is a human construct, so we should build one that helps and does not harm the human enterprise.

And in the middle of all these intellectual experiments there burst the great experiential theologies of Neo-Pentecostalism, which continue to influence the life of the international Christian community and many of the fastest-growing Christian bodies. Next we began to hear about liberation theologies that took the divine nature of Jesus very seriously and saw his redemptive work as having immediate political value and impact on the despised and oppressed of the earth. And while all this was fizzing away, there were the three great Catholic systematicians building theologies that will have enduring value: Karl Rahner, Bernard Lonergan and Hans Urs von Balthasar. Increasingly important is the eighth category of feminist theology, which could, I suppose, be seen as a subsection of liberation theology. The study of the link between theology and literature has resulted in the very interesting approach called narrative theology or the theology of story, which has been evolving contemporaneously with the new interest in Ignatian spirituality, which could be described as a kind of narrative spirituality. And finally, at number ten, is the Neo-Evangelicalism and Critique of Culture movement associated with people like Lesslie Newbigin. There have been other movements but these are enough to indicate what a turbulent and troubled mix Christian theology is. Indeed, our intellectual history is more like the politics of the Lebanon than we dare to admit; Beirut, not Upper Snodsbury, is our spiritual archetype. It is not surprising that the more alarmed among us constantly call for theological peace-keeping teams to go in and sort out the mess, an ecclesiological version of Desert Storm. The fallacy behind these authoritarian reflexes is the tranquillist heresy, the mistaken notion that turbulence is a strange aberration when, in fact, it is part of the glorious nature of a truth-seeking people; only the dead cease from troubling, the living argue.

Our fifth category, the final expression of troubled human nature, is *existential anxiety*, the troubled mind pondering the question of ultimate meaning. This is the three-o'clock-in-the-morning question, the one that catches you when hope is low and your blood is cold, and the immensities of time and space seem absurd and you yourself as insubstantial as a piece of thistledown.

Anxiety about the meaning of things troubles most human beings, but it hits with particular power against those who are professionals, executives in the meaning business. The troubles of our proud and angry dust never fail. But even in Housman's pessimism there is a releasing paradox at work. We are dust, he tells us, but mysterious dust, troubled, proud and angry dust. Housman's paradox is very like Pascal's:

> Man is only a reed, the weakest thing in nature – but a thinking
> reed. It does not take the universe in arms to crush him; a

123

vapour, a drop of water, is enough to kill him. But, though the universe should crush him, man would still be nobler than his destroyer, because he knows that he is dying, that the universe has the advantage of him; the universe knows nothing of this.[6]

And the clue to the resolution of the paradox of our magnificent frailty lies in Housman's second line. The troubles of our proud and angry dust are 'from eternity'. The turbulence in our nature is not only a mark of our human frailty, it is the stamp of eternity, the image of God in us. The narcotic longing, the tranquillist heresy, is both vain and unfaithful, because it seeks an escape from our own nature and its destiny. According to Erich Fromm, the thing that characterizes humanity is the freedom to create its own destiny. In the account given of the creation in Genesis, humanity is seen as being created in God's likeness with a capacity for an evolution of which the limits are not set. 'God', says a Hasidic master, 'does not say that "it was good" after creating man; that indicates that while the cattle and everything else were finished after being created, man was not finished.' Unlike the rest of nature, humanity is an open, not a fixed system. Humanity is an evolving being, and to be fully human is not to have a fixed set of natural characteristics, but to be on a developmental pilgrimage. Humanity is characterizied above all by a divinely gifted freedom that gives us responsibility for the fulfilment of our own nature. This godlike freedom means that, unlike the rest of creation, we are unfinished, our bounds are not fixed, and we co-create our own destiny with God. The most common human response to this divine gift is fear and repudiation. Called out again and again into the wilderness, we think only of the comforts of slavery, the fences and the fleshpots. This struggle between the unknown desert and the all-too familiar routines of Egypt characterizes every aspect of the human struggle.

No aspect of humanity's intellectual life is exempt from the pains and temptations of freedom. Christians have often tried to delude themselves into thinking that theology and morality were ring-fenced against all change, but our experience teaches us that Christianity has been a revolutionary agent in human history. Change is the law of our nature, and though it cannot be avoided it can be managed. The drama of human history consists in the struggle between rival management theories or approaches to the organization of change. In a celebrated passage in his *History of England* Macaulay observed one of the eternal human distinctions. He tells us that we find it not only in politics, about which he was speaking, but in literature, in art, in science, in surgery and mechanics, in navigation and agriculture, even in mathematics; and, we ought to add, in theology and ecclesiology. He points out that everywhere there is a group who cling with fondness to whatever is ancient and only consent to innovation with many misgivings and forebodings. And he goes on to observe another group who are always too quick to discern the imperfections of whatever exists and disposed to give every change credit for being an improvement. He points out that in the sentiments of both groups there is something to approve, but he claims that the best of both specimens will be found not far from the common frontier. The ones he detests are the extremists, what he calls bigoted dotards, in one group, and shallow and reckless empirics in the other. Reverence for what has been may moderate our progress towards what is coming to pass, but it can never stop it. Here we have no abiding city. But Paul tells us in a mysteriously mixed metaphor that we have a rock that follows us, an enduring presence in the successiveness of time that does not shackle us but, rather, in the language of both the Fourth Gospel and the Letter to the Hebrews, goes before us.

More and more in the gospels I get a sense of this active and journeying ministry of Christ and God through Christ. Christ is sent into the world. He goes into the wilderness to be tested. He sets his face to go up to Jerusalem where he tells them he is to be lifted up. He is going where they cannot yet come, but he will return and guide them into truth they cannot yet bear. After his resurrection he accompanies two of them as they trudge disconsolately towards Emmaus. Unlike other teachers he did not give us a fixed unalterable text. We know from history how dangerous these infallible manifestos are. Even as the ink

125

is drying the human enterprise has moved on and they become a far different thing to us than they were to those who wrote them or for whom they were written. This is both the danger and the opportunity of being people of a book. If the book is used as an infallible oracle that gives us orders and directs us out of difficulties, it has become a portable idol; or, to use a different symbol, a parent who will not let us grow up and upon whom we are dependent, yet whom we secretly loathe, because we know how unnatural the relationship is. The difficult life to capture, the life of grace, is the life of responsible freedom that instinctively balances itself between obedience and exploration, between reverence for the tradition and the courage to risk and be creative. This is clearly the story of parents and their children, a thing we never get entirely right, but the ideal of which we understand fairly clearly. Good parents, by their loving training of their children, enable them to leave home, to move out into the perils and challenges of adulthood. Those who are blessed in their leaving are always able to return, whereas those who are held on to long past the point of responsible love never go back as themselves, but as adults pretending to be children. The theme is obvious and prominent in literature and the life it reflects, but it is strange that we often fail to see its obvious application to religion and our relationship with the mystery we call God.

Our religious history is full of this kind of infantilism, but it is also full of rebel voices and whispered protests that call us to a true and adult spirituality. This must be part of the meaning of the mystery of the resurrection, the meaning of those mysterious words to Mary Magdalene by the risen Jesus in John's Gospel, 'Do not cling to me'; and the words to the men of Galilee on the Mount of Ascension in the Acts of the Apostles, 'Why stand you looking into heaven?' Mary and the men of Galilee had to learn a painful but liberating lesson. The divine is not to be bolted and padlocked by any of us on to any particular thing so that when we lose it we lose God. That is to make finite things into God. We are not even allowed to cling to the earthly body of Jesus. In order to know the universal spirit of Christ, the disciples had to give up, surrender the Jesus of history they had loved so much. The discomforting news that Jesus proclaimed was that the divine spirit cannot be buried in a particular tradition or system. It is forever breaking out of the prisons in which we try to contain it, bursting out of the categories in which we entomb it.

The most revolutionary thing about Christianity has always been its powerful but troubled commitment to a God whose purpose unfolds in history, to a God who is not just to be looked back at through the telescope of time past but discerned in the action of time present and the unfolding of time future. Our God does new things, does things for the first time, reveals truths hidden from previous generations and made known only unto us in these last days. The danger and paradox of our faith is that a too unyielding loyalty to the truths of our tradition can end as a disloyalty to the living God by whom previous generations were prodded into new truth. We end up as idol worshippers who are more committed to the doctrines about divine activity in the past than to a living faith in the action of God in our own time. We become custodians of a preservationist religion, a kind of religious National Trust, instead of participators in God's unfolding purpose. One only has to say that kind of thing to see how frighteningly uncertain and unsure it all is. We can have some objectivity on the past – and I say only *some*, because think how passionately we dispute even that – but how do we discern the action of God in the present? How do we know where God is leading us, what God is saying to us today? Well, we don't exactly – and that is the point. The Christian life is not an examination system in which we have to get the answers right. The Christian way is as wondrously and as adventurously inexact as life itself. We are to live it boldly, like the best generals, being more confident and hopeful of success than we are afraid of failure. This was Bonhoeffer's great insight. He called us all to the responsibility of Christian adulthood that 'depends on a God who demands responsible action in a bold venture of faith and who promises forgiveness and consolation to the man who becomes a sinner in that venture'.[7]

127

The promise of acceptance and forgiveness for us in our inexact living applies to the struggle of the intellect as much as to the struggle of the will. We do not justify ourselves either by our actions or by the polished precision of our orthodoxy. We are justified by the unconditional love God has for us in our volatile contingency and it is this basic centrality of our faith that gives us the courage to risk and to love. We love because we are first loved. We risk because God risked first, by creating us and endowing us with the freedom of the children of God. We do not have to get it right, and we will not get it right, because the Christian life is not an exact science. It is a living, evolving, kaleidoscopic, grace-filled reality and we are to live it boldy and bravely. It is through much struggle that we enter the Kingdom. And the marks of God's graced children are a loving reverence for the tradition on the one hand and an ability to risk and be creative on the other. Holding these paradoxical energies in tension is painful and acutely uncomfortable, but those are the very marks of the human enterprise. It is friction not inertia that creates energy. This used to be the mark of Anglicanism at its best. It had an inclusiveness that affirmed more than it denied. For some reason we have been taught recently to see these generous virtues as lacking that sharp-edged convincingness that impresses our type of society. Well, there clearly are things we must contend passionately for, but they should be big and generous things, things that enlarge and include people rather than diminish and exclude them. Some time ago I copied a few lines of verse from a friend's bulletin board:

> They drew a circle that shut me out –
> Heretic, rebel, a thing to flout.
> But love and I had the wit to win –
> We drew a circle that took them in.

Is not this what a truly Affirming Catholicism would do? It would bring out of its treasures things new as well as old, and it would see grace in the conflict of ideas and human types. It would draw a circle large enough to include the world that God loved so much that he sent

the divine Son into it to affirm its preciousness and die
for its freedom. Such a Church would be a church of
sinners and surprises – of sinners, because it would be for
the not already perfect. It would be for men and women
on the way, knowing something of their strength and
much about their weakness. It would be a Church big
enough to hold the ones whose ritual status is allegedly
not quite perfect, because they have failed some test of
acceptability, by their marital or sexual status, or by their
inability or refusal to see the point of pretending to exact
knowledge of the unknowable mystery that besets us, yet
who want to accompany the tradition and, above all, share
its experience of prayer and silence. But above all it would
be a Church of surprises because it knew that God had
not finished yet and no grave can hold the divine.

I have only recently discovered the poetry of Louis Mac-
Neice. Let me end by quoting from a poem of his called
'Mutations':

If there has been no spiritual change of kind
Within our species since Cro-Magnon man,
And none is looked for now, while the millennia cool,
Yet each of us has known mutations of the mind,
When the world jumped, and what had been a plan
Dissolved, and rivers ran from what had been a pool.

For every static world that you or I impose
Upon the real one must crack at times, and new
Patterns from new disorders open like a rose,
And old assumptions yield to new sensation
The stranger in the wings is waiting for his cue
The fuse is always laid to some annunciation.

Surprises keep us living: as when the first light
Surprised our infant eyes, or as when, very small
Clutching our parents' hands we toddled down a road
Where all was blank and windless both to touch and sight
Had we not suddenly raised our eyes, which showed
The long grass growing wild on top of the high wall.

For it is true, surprises break and make
As when the baton falls, and all together the hands

On the fiddle bows are pistons, or when, crouched above
His books the scholar suddenly understands
What he has thought for years – or when the inveterate rake
Finds for once that his lust is becoming love.[8]

1 A.E. Housman, 'Epigraph' to *More Poems*, 1936.
2 From 'The Chestnut Casts His Flambeaux' in A.E. Housman, *Poetry and Prose: a Selection*, ed. F.C. Norwood (Hutchinson, 1971).
3 Peter Brown, *Augustine of Hippo* (Faber, 1967), p. 246.
4 Philip Larkin, 'This Be the Verse' in *High Windows* (Faber, 1974).
5 Norman F. Nixon, *The Psychology of Military Incompetence* (Futura, 1988).
6 *The Oxford Book of Death* (Oxford University Press, 1983), p. 40.
7 Dietrich Bonhoeffer, *Letters and Papers from Prison* (SCM Press 1967), p. 29.
8 Louis MacNeice, 'Mutations' in *Collected Poems* (Faber, 1966).

Epilogue: Catholicism and the Living Christ*

John Habgood

> Jesus said, 'All authority in heaven and on earth has been given to me. Go, therefore, make disciples of all the nations; baptize them in the name of the Father and of the Son and of the Holy Spirit, and teach them to observe all the commands I gave you. And know that I am with you always; yes, to the end of time.' (Matthew 28:18–20)

'All authority . . . all nations . . . all commands . . . all time . . . ' The vision of universality runs all the way through these closing verses of St Matthew. The gospel is for all, about all, comprehending all, and it is the measure of the stature of the fullness of Christ that he is the foundation stone on which the whole of God's building rests. These are huge claims: huge at the time they were first made when the Church was a tiny insignificant group of Jewish dissidents; and huge today when we can no longer ignore the facts of religious and cutural pluralism and when divisions reach right down into the heart of the Christian community.

Yet universality is not an optional extra for Christians. Our faith is either about everything or it is about some private world of our own. In fact anyone who takes belief in God seriously has to have something of the same universal vision.

I came across these words recently: 'The mission is for

*© John Habgood, 1991. A sermon preached in York Minster at the end of the Affirming Catholicism conference.

131

the whole world . . . we all know that it cannot be stopped . . . because this is the mission in which God is working himself . . . ' Part of a handout for the Decade of Evangelism? No. Part of an exhortation to a tiny Sikh sect whose leader was murdered in Britain in 1987. The writer saw no absurdity in making such a claim, and neither should we. Anyone less than the Lord of all the earth is not 'the God and Father of our Lord Jesus Christ'. This is where Catholicism begins. Those of us who want to call ourselves Catholics do so because our commitment is not to a merely private faith but to universal truth.

But that truth has to be embodied before it can be grasped, and this is of course where our troubles begin. Christ the foundation – we are agreed on that. Christ the touchstone of where God's truth lies – that too we all accept. Christ the hidden reality, often unperceived in the richness and variety of our pluralist world and in a divided church – some find that concept harder to take hold of than others.

An affirmative Catholicism, it seems to me, has always tried to reach out and identify Christ's presence everywhere in a great sacramental overspill. And in so doing it has somehow affirmed the world, and life, and liveliness. Remember Dag Hammarskjöld:

> I don't know who or what put the question. I don't know when it was put. I don't even remember answering. But at some moment I did answer Yes to Someone – or Something – and from that hour I was certain that existence is meaningful and that, therefore, my life, in self-surrender, had a goal.[1]

Was this Christ at work? Dare one see echoes, too, in something as unlikely as the final great Yes at the end of James Joyce's Ulysses? Contrast with this what Dr Johnson said about George I: 'George the First knew nothing, and desired to know nothing; did nothing and desired to do nothing; and the only good thing that is told of him is that he wished to restore the crown to its hereditary successor.'[2] 'Affirming Catholicism' means in part, I hope, the kind of Catholicism which affirms, the kind of Catholicism which makes life difficult for ecclesiastical George the

Firsts – if such there be – the kind of Catholicism which reaches out and seeks to embrace the world.

Yet in his one good quality, as perceived by Dr Johnson, George had a clear sense of the importance of continuity. Without a strong and continuing central core of meaning to hold it together, affirmation is liable to become indiscriminate, and thereby slide into vacuousness. Embodiment entails succession, as kings have every reason to know, and even the most affirmative body needs to know where its central core of meaning lies, and how far this can change and develop in the light of changing circumstances. It is a question to which our Christian faith gives its own special answer. The Christian core of meaning lies not in some doctrine or structure, but in a story, a set of events, a person and a relationship. In a word, in Christ.

It is this which gives the Christian faith flexibility and variety, and which makes it genuinely universal. Doctrinal formulae and particular structures belong to particular times and cultures and mindsets. Stories, events and relationships can generate meaning in any time or any culture, and so, paradoxically, it is precisely the historical rootedness of Christianity which enables it to be transplanted into so many different soils. Universality is possible, in other words, precisely because we take seriously the particularity of our historical tradition centred on Christ.

But this still leaves us with the question, how do we maintain and develop that tradition? What sort of defences do we need to safeguard the central core of meaning? When do we stop saying 'Yes' and start saying 'No'? Here, I think, some words of Adrian Hastings can help us. First a warning which he takes from the poet David Jones, a warning against dismantling and amalgamating too easily 'till everything presuming difference and all the sweet remembered demarcations wither to the touch of us . . . '[3] Embodied faith loves and cherishes its particular forms, and if we have learnt anything from the conservative reaction in these last decades it must surely be that we impoverish ourselves if we throw away 'sweet remembered demarcations' without an awareness of what is being lost.

The other side of the coin Hastings puts helpfully like this:

> If changes are merely culture-controlled, they are fairly sure to be bad changes, if significant at all. The guarantee of their appropriateness must be that they express organically the central core of the tradition within an altered cultural context. The heart of the meaning within the tradition remains, the periphery changes because in the new circumstances the old periphery would be a disservice to the heart.[4]

In other words, the developments we have to make in our traditions are developments which are essential if we are to remain faithful to the core of it. And that core, as I have said, is a story, a set of events, a person, the particularities which make the universality of the Gospel possible. If stubborn adherence to tradition begins, as it were, to lock Christ into some cultural form which falsifies the essential gospel message and denies its universality, then faithfulness to the past ceases to be faithfulness to God.

'All authority has been given to me . . . go therefore, make disciples of all nations.' Not the authority of empire. Not the authority of some supposedly infallible truth. Not authority defined in fixed words and structures. But the authority of a living presence, promised to us always; a living presence still discernible through the murkiness and ambiguities of history, and the many failures of those who lay claim to his name; a living presence again and again made real to us, in the Body, through the Body, broken and given to us as the pledge of eternal reality.

1 Dag Hammarskjöld, *Markings* (Faber, 1964), entry for Whitsunday 1961.
2 James Boswell, *Life of Samuel Johnson*, entry for 6 April 1775.
3 Adrian Hastings, *The Theology of a Protestant Catholic* (SCM Press, 1990), p. 87.
4 Ibid., p. 94.

Note on
Affirming Catholicism

The Affirmation movement has never been and is not intended to be yet another 'party' within the Church of England or the Anglican Communion.

Following the conference in York in July 1991, an application was lodged with the Charity Commissioners with the intention of achieving charitable status for Affirming Catholicism and its publishing outlet, *Mainstream*. The following is extracted from the draft document:

> It is the conviction of many that a respect for scholarship and free enquiry has been characteristic of the Church of England and of the Churches of the wider Anglican Communion from earliest times and is fully consistent with the status of those Churches as part of the Holy Catholic Church. It is desired to establish a charitable educational foundation which will be true both to those characteristics and to the Catholic tradition within Anglicanism . . .
>
> . . . The object of the foundation shall be the advancement of education in the doctrines and the historical development of the Church of England and the Churches of the wider Anglican Communion, as held by those professing to stand within the Catholic tradition.
>
> The intention is:
>
> 1. To organise or support lectures, conferences and seminars.
>
> 2. To publish or support books, tracts, journals and other written material.
>
> 3. To provide resources for local groups of supporters of the foundation meeting for purposes of study and discussion.

The Steering Committee consists of:

> Mr Lewis Ayres
> The Revd Canon Michael Banks
> The Revd Dr Lida Ellsworth
> The Revd Preb. John Gaskell
> The Rt Revd Richard Holloway
> The Revd David Hutt
> The Revd Dr Jeffrey John
> The Revd Nerissa Jones
> Mr Martin Lawrence
> The Very Revd Dr John Moses
> The Rt Revd Jack Nicholls
> The Revd Victor Stock
> Dame Rachel Waterhouse
> The Revd Professor Rowan Williams

Enquiries regarding the aims and activities of Affirming Catholicism together with its publications and future programme may be addessed to:

> Elizabeth Field
> St Mary-le-Bow
> Cheapside
> London EC2V 6AU